Bible Puzzles, Quizzes & Brain Twisters

The **BIG FUN** variety collection

Inspired by Faith

Bible Puzzles, Quizzes & Brain Twisters
ISBN 978-0-9895802-3-6

Published by Product Concept Mfg., Inc.
2175 N. Academy Circle #200, Colorado Springs, CO 80909

All scripture quotations are from the King James version of the Bible unless otherwise noted.

Answers based on common translations of the Bible. Where translations differ, refer to the Authorized (King James) Version.

BIBLE PUZZLES, QUIZZES & BRAIN TWISTERS

A wise man will hear,

and will increase learning...

Proverbs 1:5

SHARPEN UP YOUR BIBLE KNOWLEDGE!

These challenging and fun puzzles will not only refresh your memory of the bible–you might learn some surprising new facts, too! The big fun variety collection of word search puzzles, crosswords, brain twisters and more will keep you entertained for hours.

Miraculous!

During His earthly ministry, Jesus performed many miracles to show His power over natural forces. In the word search below, nine of these miracles can be found, each one consisting of two intersecting words. Words read left to right; top to bottom. Cover the word box and see how many you can find without peeking!

LAZARUS RAISED

LEPERS HEALED

LAME WALKED

MUTE SPOKE

SEA CALMED

EYES SAW

DEAF HEARD

WATER [changed to] WINE

CROWD FED

H E A R D M O R E D O N
Q U N A E B I R K S N I
N L A Z A R U S N A O M
N E A R F A N E C C L E
S H E P H I C A L M E D
N O L B O S Y E W C R O
T H E A L E D M A J O B
A N P L C D E A L O N A
E Y E S R A S E K W O W
T H R A O L A M E A B A
C O S W W E H U D Y E T
O N F E D A N T W I N E
T H E S P O K E C O O R

Answers are in the back of the book.

It's in the Good Book

Test your Bible knowledge by marking these familiar sayings True if they are derived from the Bible, and False if not from the Bible.

1. T F God helps those who help themselves.
2. T F A drop in the bucket.
3. T F Silence is golden.
4. T F Pride goes before the fall.
5. T F Tell the truth and shame the devil.
6. T F Fools jump in where angels fear to tread.
7. T F A penny saved is a penny earned.
8. T F By the skin of your teeth.
9. T F Honesty is the best policy.
10. T F Where there's smoke, there's fire.
11. T F Neither a borrower nor a lender be.
12. T F A little bird told me.

Answers are in the back of the book.

Names Of Jesus Word Search

Almighty	Comforter	King of Kings
Alpha and Omega	Creator	The Life
Author	Eternal Father	Messiah
Beloved	Shepherd	Redeemer
Carpenter	Healer	Son Of God
Christ	Holy One	The Word

```
U Y H N V E R E D E E M E R I J
N Y V W S C O B H O Y F E Y D D
H F E S H X Z A O M L K I H U R
Y K T R C E I W Q A L O M O E O
H E I T G S T H E L I F E L A W
C S T N S F D S A M W E A Y G E
T O R E G Y H N I I A E L O E H
D L M B R O Y F E G H S X N M T
E R F F G N F R O H T U A E O K
V R P K O M A K G T U B H Y D S
O E O S X R O L I Y D P F M N O
L E N T G T T N F N Y B I M A N
E R V E A U Y E T A G F M N A O
B V W O M E K L R L T S V N H F
Y G T F R D R E H P E H S H P G
R V E D U N T C R V R D E S L O
N C A R P E N T E R P O M R A D
```

Answers are in the back of the book.

Ties That Bind

Each group of Bible people shares something in common. From the list below, match the names with the ties that bind them!

DISCIPLES	FISHERMEN	KINGS
MISSIONARIES	NOAH'S SONS	PRIESTS
PROPHETS	SIBLINGS	FAMILY MEMBERS

1. SAUL, DAVID, SOLOMON ________________
2. PETER, JOHN, JAMES ________________
3. DEBORAH, HULDAH, ANNA ________________
4. SHEM, HAM, JAPHETH ________________
5. AARON, MIRIAM, MOSES ________________
6. ELI, AHIMAAZ, MELCHIZEDEK ________________
7. NAOMI, RUTH, ORPAH ________________
8. ANDREW, SIMON PETER, JOHN ________________
9. PAUL, SILAS, BARNABAS ________________

Answers are in the back of the book.

Plant a Tree

A grower couldn't decide what kind of tree to plant, so he planted a variety of trees in his orchard! See if you can find these trees mentioned in the Bible.

FIR	CEDAR	FIG
OAK	ACACIA	PALM
BRAMBLE	APPLE	SYCAMORE
ALMOND	OLIVE	

B	E	A	P	L	A	I	N	E	E	D	S	O
R	A	N	A	L	M	O	N	D	X	O	Y	U
A	C	U	L	A	M	L	C	R	E	N	C	T
M	H	C	M	P	E	I	A	O	M	O	A	K
B	R	O	O	M	T	V	B	A	P	L	M	Y
L	U	A	P	P	L	E	E	C	L	I	O	T
E	R	M	I	E	M	A	O	A	F	I	R	I
M	T	I	S	X	F	L	M	C	I	V	E	M
E	A	O	I	I	N	F	E	I	G	E	A	E
V	M	M	C	E	D	A	R	A	D	D	M	T

Answers are in the back of the book.

Bible Scribes

Fit the names of Bible authors in the grid below, crossing off the names as you fit them in. The first name has been added to get you started.

4 letters	5 letters	6 letters	7 letters
AMOS	DAVID	DANIEL	EZEKIEL
EZRA	JAMES	ISAIAH	SOLOMON
~~JOEL~~	MICAH	JOSHUA	**8 letters**
JOHN	MOSES		HABAKKUK
LUKE	NAHUM		JEREMIAH
MARK	PETER		
PAUL			

J
O
E
L

Answers are in the back of the book.

Who's Guilty

Pick the culprit in the lineup!

1. **He led a revolt against Moses.**

   (a) Caleb (b) Goliath (c) Korah (d) Joshua

2. **He wanted to kill David.**

   (a) Saul (b) Paul (c) Doeg (d) Cain

3. **This king of Judah sacrificed his children to idols.**

   (a) David (b) Ahaz (c) Ahab (d) Josiah

4. **His planned massacre was averted.**

   (a) Pashur (b) Ahab (c) Joab (d) Haman

5. **He ordered John the Baptist beheaded.**

   (a) Pilate (b) Herod

   (c) Annas (d) Caiaphas

6. **He betrayed His Lord.**

   (a) Judas Priest (b) Judas Iscariot

   (c) Judas Barsabas (d) Judas the brother of James

Answers are in the back of the book.

Look Again!

There are 5 subtle differences between these two pictures. Can you find them?

"I have good news and bad news. The good news is we have enough money for the new church roof. The bad news is... it's still in your pockets."

Beatitudes Word Search

You'll recognize these words and phrases from the familiar scriptures. Find and circle all those highlighted words in the word search puzzle.

- Blessed are the **poor in spirit**, for theirs is the **kingdom of heaven**.
- Blessed are **those who mourn**, for they will be **comforted**.
- Blessed are the **meek**, for they will **inherit the earth**.
- Blessed are those who **hunger and thirst** after **righteousness**, for they will be filled.
- Blessed are the **merciful**, for they shall be shown mercy.
- Blessed are the **pure in heart**, for **they will see God**.
- Blessed are the **peacemakers**, for they will be called **children of God**.
- Blessed are those **who are persecuted** because of righteousness, for theirs is the kingdom of heaven.
- **Blessed are** you when people insult you, persecute you and falsely say all kinds of evil against you because of me.
- Rejoice and be glad, because **great is your reward** in heaven, for in the same way they persecuted the prophets who were before you.

Matthew 5:3-12 NIV

Answers are in the back of the book.

U Y C H I L D R E N O F G O D J

E T U C E S R E P K O T B G Y N

H F E S Q X Z P T M I K I J U E

P E A C E M A K E R S O M I N V

H B Y T G V T F I E O C I M O A

L K J H G F D P A Q W F R T V E

E C R D T Y S N I P M O M M I H

P L O H R N Y F E U W S X O E F

V R F T I R M U J R N T G B C O

O L P R G U Y N G E U G H Y V M

P E O A H O D F A I D R F M I O

F O N E T M W N O N Y E I M T D

P R V E E O Y N T H A A M S V G

D V W H O H K L P E T T R N B N

O G T T U W E S W A Q I M H I I

G V E T S E T C R R H S M E E K

E T F I N S G H J T P Y M U I O

E Y H R E O X W D Y N O L M I J

S Y V E S H D N U K O U B G Y N

L F E H S T A P O M I R I J U E

L B T N C R S W Q R L R M I N V

I B Y I E V T F I E D E I M O A

W K J G G F D P A Q W W R T V E

Y C N D B L E S S E D A R E I H

E U O B G N L U F I C R E M E F

H R F B I T M U J Y N D G B I O

T H P R I M Y N G B U B H Y V M

W H O A R E P E R S E C U T E D

What Is It?

Test your knowledge by circling the correct definition of these words associated with the Bible:

1. **MITE:** a. Tree b. Coin c. Fish
2. **MANNA:** a. Desert b. Bush c. Food
3. **BAAL:** a. Altar b. Idol c. Haystack
4. **PENTATEUCH:** a. First five books
   b. Tongues of fire event c. Satanic symbol
5. **JUDAH:** a. Holy Land Kingdom
   b. Betrayer of Jesus c. Branch of the Jordon River
6. **PARABLE:** a. Song b. Idea c. Story
7. **ALMS:** a. Variety of dates b. Beasts of burden
   c. Money to the poor
8. **ESCHATOLOGY:** a. Study of End Times
   b. Doctrine of original sin c. Study of miracles
9. **EPISTLE:** a. Weed b. Female apostle c. Letter
10. **SABBATH:** a. Day of rest b. City of refuge c. Show of strength
11. **LOGOS:** a. Toy b. Word c. Wood
12. **TIMBREL:** a. Musical instrument b. Tableware
    c. Sewing accessory

Answers are in the back of the book.

Hint, Hint...

In this word search, you'll find the highlighted words from the previous page along with their correct definitions.

T R O P L M N U Y H T A R F E D
S T F B R D E W S X A L A A B N
T U T J P T B O P L M M U Y N Y
U B N F M E L M E P I S T L E P
D U E I A N N T B R C E W E Q S
Y L M B N C E T G S D I Y T T M
O Y U V N W Q F A M E N Y T V O
F G R W A B U B E T B T R E Y N
E O T W S X B O I R E E M R M E
N L S C D A W M I Y T U T B O Y
D O N I T Y T B R I V A C P D T
T T I H J L P O M N I O S H G O
I A L L E R B M I T F E O R N T
M H A D U J N O L I M P G O I H
E C C H B T C V E O D B O N K E
S S I N H U J P A R A B L E D P
B E S C F D A Y O F R E S T N O
H B U T G O T W R E D K I M A O
L K M H G F O S S Q W E O T L R
E C R D T Y H D I T M O L L Y K
F I R S T F I V E B O O K S L D
V R F B G T M U J Y N R G B O K
O L P K I I D O L B U B Y Y H R

Men Of The Bible Word Search

Abel	Samson	Daniel
Noah	Samuel	John The Baptist
Abraham	Saul	Jesus
Job	David	Peter
Moses	Elijah	Paul
Joshua	Jonah	

```
Y G T S I T P A B E H T N H O J
R V E D U N T C R V R D E H M I
N T F E L T G H J L J O A U I O
U Y J N U E X W D Y N O L M I J
N J O N A H D C U K N H S G Y N
H F B S P X Z P O M L K I H U N
Y B T V C E S W O A L O M I U H
H B Y T S A M S O N L C I M O A
L J J H G F E S A E W E R T V J
E C E D T S H N U J M O L M I I
P L O S G T Y M E C W S X C E L
V L F B U M A H A R B A G R I E
O U P K I S Y N G B U B E Y V R
D A V I D A D F A K E T F M I P
F S N U G T D A N I E L I M O L
Y R V E O U Y N T P A F M N V C
D V W O M I K L P L T G V N B H
```

Answers are in the back of the book.

Word Play

Build as many Bible-related words as you can from the word Scripture, with each word sharing at least one letter with another word. The puzzle has been started for you.

Answers will vary.

Bible Timeline

Put these events in order as they took place in Bible history:

____ Solomon's Temple is built

____ John the Baptist is born

____ Noah builds an Ark

____ Jesus dies on Calvary and rises on the third day

____ Abraham goes to the Promised Land

____ The Apostle John receives visions of End Times

____ Paul spreads the Gospel during wide-ranging missionary trips

____ Joseph is taken to Egypt

____ King David rules in Jerusalem

____ Gabriel brings a message to Mary

____ God places Adam and Eve in the Garden of Eden

____ Jesus teaches throughout Galilee and Judea

____ Ten Commandments are given to Moses on Mount Sinai

____ Jesus is baptized

Answers are in the back of the book.

Hidden Disciples

The names of seven of Jesus' disciples are hidden in the sentences below. Can you spot them?

I can't stop for this, I'm on a schedule!

____

If you get in a jam, escape to Philippi!

____

Matt hewed the tree with one blow of his ax.

____

For a pet, Erica chose a calico cat.

____

Be kind and rewind.

____

Johnnycakes are her specialty.

____

Answers are in the back of the book.

God's Promise - When You Need Direction

Cross out one letter of each pair to reveal God's promise to you in the book of Proverbs, chapter 3.

IT HN EA CL AL GT OH DY SW MA OY AS LA

BC KI BN LO EW LE EY ID SG WE OH IW MO,

RA DN AD NH DE GS OH SA PL LE LD AI MR

FE EC TP TA OH LY JP EA ST HU ES.

Write your answer below.

____,

____.

Proverbs 3: _____

Answer is in the back of the book.

Bible Match Ups

Match the name in the first column with the right name in the second column!

Couples

1. Zacharias	a. Herodias
2. Hosea	b. Ruth
3. Herod	c. Salome
4. Aquila	d. Elizabeth
5. Boaz	e. Sapphira
6. Zebedee	f. Priscilla
7. Ananias	g. Gomer

Mothers and Sons

1. Bathsheba	a. Jesus
2. Rachel	b. John the Baptist
3. Mary	c. Solomon
4. Eunice	d. Samuel
5. Hannah	e. Jacob
6. Elizabeth	f. Timothy
7. Rebekah	g. Joseph

Answer is in the back of the book.

What Do You Know About the Bible?

Pick the correct answer from the choices given!

1. The first five books of the Bible:
a. Gospels b. Pentateuch c. Epistles

2. The first four books of the New Testament:
a. Gospels b. Pentateuch c. Epistles

3. The Lord's Prayer can be found in:
a. Exodus b. Matthew c. Corinthians

4. The 10 Commandments can be found in:
a. Genesis b. Exodus c. Haggai

5. The relationship of God to His people is described as:
a. Zookeeper to animals b. Weaver to cloth
c. Shepherd to sheep

6. The Garden of Eden is introduced in:
a. Genesis b. Luke c. Acts

7. **Not a parable of Jesus:**

a. Prodigal Son b. Good Samaritan
c. Hare and the Tortoise

8. **The last book of the Bible is:**

a. Malachi b. Revelation c. Thessalonians

9. **Not a book in the New Testament:**

a. Malachi b. Revelation c. Thessalonians

10. **Epistle means:**

a. History b. Letter c. E-document

11. **"The Prayer Book of the Bible" is:**

a. Genesis b. Corinthians c. Psalms

12. **The "Great Love Chapter" of the Bible is found in:**

a. Genesis b. Corinthians c. Psalms

Answer is in the back of the book.

God's Promise - When You Wonder Where He Is

Cross out words according to the instructions to reveal a Bible truth.

BREAD DOVE LO ANTS CORN I JOB AM EARTH

OWLS AWAY FLOUR LUKE CAMEL WITH OLIVES

YOU SERPENT IN HEAVEN RUTH FRUIT A ALWAYS

FIGS MANGER NUMBERS

Cross out...

1. all books of the Bible.
2. words that form the title of a well-known Christmas carol.
3. the two things God created in the beginning.
4. food items
5. animals

Answer:

____

Answers are in the back of the book.

Name Above All Names

Unscrambled the words to form names for Jesus Christ found in the Bible.

1. S H A S I E M

___ ___ ___ ___ ___ ___ ___

2. R A Z E A N N E

___ ___ ___ ___ ___ ___ ___ ___

3. E E E E R M R D

___ ___ ___ ___ ___ ___ ___ ___

4. R A M O D I E T

___ ___ ___ ___ ___ ___ ___ ___

5. S E R O C O N U L

___ ___ ___ ___ ___ ___ ___ ___ ___

6. L A P A H

___ ___ ___ ___ ___

7. A M E N L U M E

___ ___ ___ ___ ___ ___ ___ ___

Answers are in the back of the book.

Women of the Bible

Choose the correct woman's name for each of these descriptions.

1. She heard God's first promise of a Savior.
   a. Eve
   b. Mary
   c. Martha

2. She gave thanks upon seeing the baby Jesus.
   a. Elizabeth
   b. Miriam
   c. Anna

3. Peter raised her from the dead.
   a. Judith
   b. Anna
   c. Tabitha

4. She had 12 brothers.
   a. Deborah
   b. Dinah
   c. Dorcas

5. She remained faithful to her mother-in-law, Naomi.
   a. Orpah
   b. Ruth
   c. Tamar

6. She was a prophetess consulted by priests and elders.
   a. Huldah
   b. Hannah
   c. Heidi

7. Jesus appeared to her after His resurrection.
   a. Salome
   b. Joanne
   c. Mary Magdalene

Answers are in the back of the book.

Bible Vocabulary

How well do you know the meaning of words that appear in the Bible? Test yourself by circling the best definition!

1. COMMANDMENT
   a. advice
   b. law
   c. suggestion

2. EBENEZER
   a. The Lord has helped us
   b. God is merciful
   c. He has redeemed His people

3. CHRIST
   a. Teacher
   b. Rabbi
   c. Messiah

4. SILOAM
   a. Sent
   b. Peace
   c. Health

5. SABBATH
   a. Day of punishment
   b. Day of birth
   c. Day of rest

6. COMFORTER
   a. Jesus Christ
   b. Holy Spirit
   c. God Almighty

7. JUSTIFIED
   a. Punished by God
   b. Brought near God
   c. Made right with God

8. EPISTLE
   a. Bramble
   b. Letter
   c. Wife of an apostle

Answers are in the back of the book.

All About God Crossword

ACROSS

1 Shows mercy
4 Consoles
7 Not wicked
9 Loyal
10 Restores
11 Delivers
13 Old Testament name
15 Immutable
19 Here now
20 Always was, always will be
22 Maker
23 All-knowing
24 Listens
26 Without error
27 Fair
28 Makes known

DOWN

1 One person of Godhead
2 Second person of Godhead
3 God is ___
5 Three-in-one
6 Mighty
8 His kingdom
12 Compassionate
14 Third person of Godhead (2 words)
16 Confers happiness
17 Not of earth
18 Instructs
19 Vows
21 Gives this to us
25 Observes

Answers are in the back of the book.

Look Again!

There are 5 subtle differences between these two pictures. Can you find them?

You can tell the regular churchgoers because if they're missing a spoon, salad bowl, or casserole dish, the first place they look is in the church kitchen.

CHURCH POTLUCK
TONIGHT

Ridin' Along

In the list below, find the right vehicle for each rider.

LADDER	CHARIOT	ARK	HORSE
CAMEL	FISH	BOAT	COLT

1. Noah weathered a storm in one.

   ____

2. Jesus entered Jerusalem on one.

   ____

3. The Ethiopian invited Philip to hop right in.

   ____

4. Peter stepped out of his, then wished he hadn't.

   ____

5. Jonah was an unwilling passenger in one.

   ____

6. Jacob saw angels using one in a dream.

   ____

7. Rebekah rode one on her way to meet Isaac.

   ____

8. A rider rode a white one in the book of Revelation.

   ____

Answers are in the back of the book.

Who's Older?

Put these Bible names in order of when they were born, from earliest to latest. The first one has been done for you.

A. 3 Esther
5 Dorcas
1 Eve
4 Mary Magdalene
2 Hannah

B. ___Paul
___Jacob
___Abel
___Matthew
___Noah

C. ___King Herod
___Timothy
___Jesus
___Amos
___Lot

D. ___Luke
___David
___Joshua
___Micah
___Solomon

Answer is in the back of the book.

Prophets Of The Bible Word Search

Amos	Hosea	Micah
Daniel	Isaiah	Nahum
Elijah	Jeremiah	Obadiah
Ezekiel	Joel	Samuel
Habakkuk	Jonah	Zephaniah
Haggai	Malachi	

E C Z E P H A N I A H O L M I K
P L O B G T Y H A C I M X C E D
V R L B G T M U J Y N T G B H K
O J E R E M I A H E U B H Y I R
P O I S X A D F Z K L P F M S P
F E N U G T W E O U Y I I M A L
Y L A M O S K N T H A F J N I C
D V D O M I K L P A R G O A A H
U Y H N E E X M D B N N N M H J
N Y V L S I A G G A H H A G Y N
S A M U E L Z P O K L K H H U N
Y B T V A E S W Q K L O M I U U
H B Y C G V T F R U D C I M O M
L K H H G F D S A K W E R T V R
Y I T F R D O B A D I A H H I Y
R V H O S E A C R V R D E S M I
N T F E Y T G H J L P O M U I O

Answers are in the back of the book.

Book List

See how well you know your Bible stats! Pick the right answer for each question.

1. What is the longest book of the Bible? (Hint: It has 150 chapters!)
   a. Psalms b. Proverbs c. Revelation

2. How many Gospels are there in the New Testament?
   a. Four b. Six c. Eight

3. How many books are in the KJV Bible?
   a. 64 b. 66 c. 68

4. Who's the oldest person mentioned in the Bible?
   a. Melchizedek b. Malachi c. Methuselah

5. Which is the shortest of these books of the bible?
   a. Philemon b. 2 John c. Jude

6. Who in the Bible traveled the most extensively?
   a. Abraham b. Paul c. Jesus

7. Who's the person, other than Jesus, mentioned the most number of times in the Bible?
   a. Adam b. Moses c. David

Answers are in the back of the book.

Pyramid Play

Help the Children of Israel build Pharaoh's pyramid by thinking of words of increasing length using the letters provided.

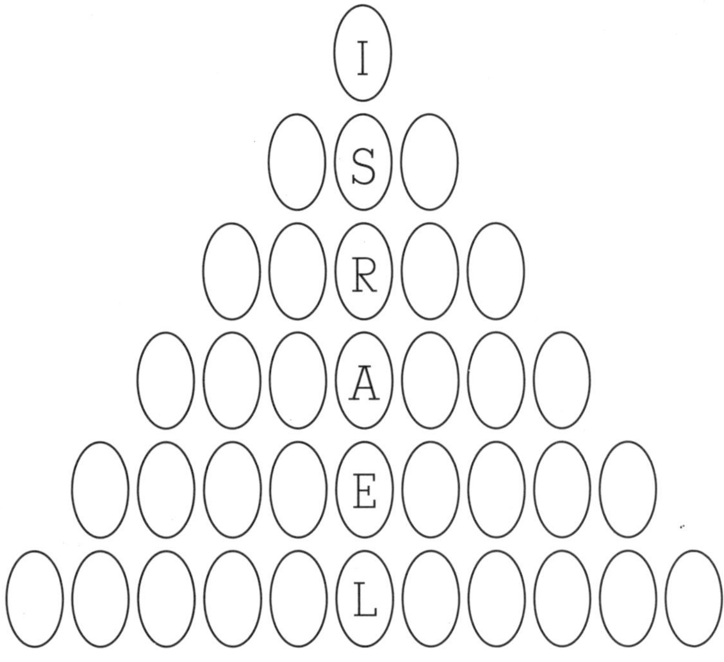

Possible answers are in the back of the book.

Jacob's Kids

Jacob's 12 sons* and one daughter are missing. Can you find them? Here's the challenge: their names appear right to left; left to right; top to bottom; bottom to top; and on the diagonal!
*These became the twelve tribes of Israel.

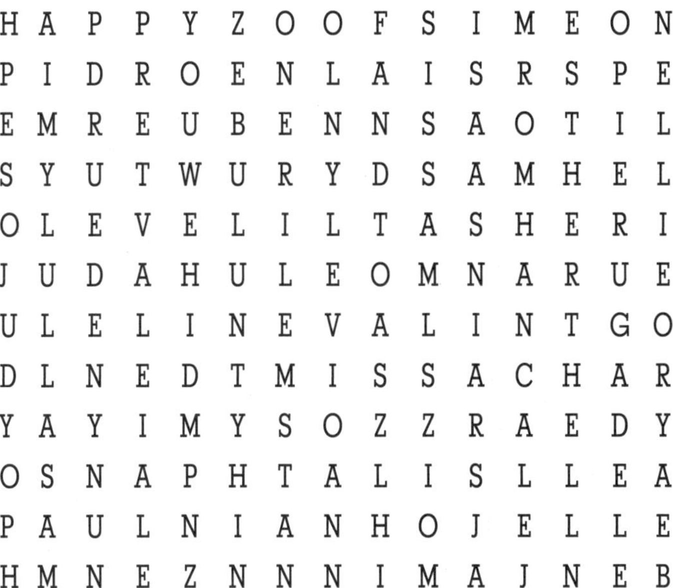

H A P P Y Z O O F S I M E O N
P I D R O E N L A I S R S P E
E M R E U B E N N S A O T I L
S Y U T W U R Y D S A M H E L
O L E V E L I L T A S H E R I
J U D A H U L E O M N A R U E
U L E L I N E V A L I N T G O
D L N E D T M I S S A C H A R
Y A Y I M Y S O Z Z R A E D Y
O S N A P H T A L I S L L E A
P A U L N I A N H O J E L L E
H M N E Z N N N I M A J N E B

Hint: Genesis 35:23-26; 30:21

Answers are in the back of the book.

Bible Animals Crossword

ACROSS

2 The devil is like a roaring one

4 Plague hoppers

6 We're like them

10 They will be separated from 6 Across

11 Noah sent one out of the ark

12 Honey providers

14 "Go to the __, thou sluggard" (Prov. 6:6 kjv)

15 Big sea creature

18 Sacrificial animal

20 Symbol for the Holy Spirit

22 Associated with Peter's denial

23 Jesus compared King Herod to one (Luke 13:32 kjv)

DOWN

1 What Peter wanted to catch

2 Plague pests

3 John the Baptizer's chosen foods

5 Not one falls without God's knowledge

6 Eden tempter

7 The prodigal son fed them

8 Manna supplement

9 Jesus rode into Jerusalem on one

13 Riches "fly away as an ___ toward heaven" (Prov. 23:5 kjv)

16 Apocalypse gallopers

17 It ate Jonah's shade plant

19 John the Baptizer wore the hair of one

21 Jesus compares a false prophet to one

Answers are in the back of the book.

Bible Places

Can you name these Bible places? Watch out–some are harder than others!

1. Where the walls came tumbling down.

 ____

2. Where the languages were confused.

 ____

3. Jesus spent His boyhood here.

 ____

4. Paul was born here.

 ____

5. John Mark left Paul and went home from here.

 ____

6. Ruth came from here.

 ____

7. After the Resurrection, some disciples decided to walk here.

 ____

8. King David ruled from this city.

 ____

9. Jonah hoped God would destroy this city.

 ____

10. Cain built this city.

 ____

Answers are in the back of the book.

Good Food, Let's Eat!

Choose the correct answer–and bon appetit!

1. Jesus compared the kingdom of heaven to this seed.

   a) Poppy b) Mustard c) Coriander d) Flower

2. Ruth gleaned the fields of Boaz during these harvests.

   a) Corn and maize b) Cocoa and coffee

   c) Soybeans and wheat d) Wheat and barley

3. Jesus saw Nathanael under a tree that bears these.

   a) Figs b) Olives c) Apples d) Dates

4. John the Baptist made these a staple of his diet.

   a) Wasps b) Katydids c) Scorpions d) Locusts

5. At the Last Supper, Jesus blessed these.

   a) Bread and wine b) Milk and honey

   c) Barley cakes and water d) Apples and oranges

6. Jesus fed a multitude of more than 5000 with these.

   a) 7 loaves and 3 fish b) 5 loaves and 2 fish

   c) 2 loaves and 7 fish d) 12 loaves and 1 fish

Answers are in the back of the book.

Bible Men Crossword

ACROSS

2 One of 12 brothers
4 Wicked king of the Old Testament
6 He "walked with God" (Gen. 5:22 kjv)
7 1 Down brother
8 NT physician
11 Betrayer
14 God changed his name to Israel
16 Companion of 24 Across
17 Judge at Jesus' trial
19 Patriarch
20 24 Across brother
23 Epistle writer
24 Commandment receiver
25 Ark builder
26 NT king
27 OT king
28 Savior

DOWN

1 5 Down son
2 Gospel writer
3 Israel's first king
5 First man
6 Prophet pursued by 4 Across
9 Tax collector turned disciple
10 Believing Pharisee
12 Went to Tarsus to look for Paul
13 Fisherman turned disciple
15 Eunice's missionary son
18 Raised from the dead
21 19 Across son
22 A fish swallowed him

Answers are in the back of the book.

By the Book

Fourteen books of the Bible are hidden in this paragraph. Can you find them all? Underline your answers.

He who judges, the Bible says, will be himself judged, so the ruthless man repented of his evil acts. "Just look at the numbers!" he remarked in loud lamentations when he realized what a jam, estranged from God, he was in. "This is a revelation to me, and now I want to do a better job." He regrets he was lacking so much in wisdom, and now the man sings praises, psalms, and follows wise proverbs. He is not lukewarm, but firmly believes there is forgiveness in Jesus.

Answers are in the back of the book.

Nine-Patch Puzzler

Rearrange the squares to spell the name of a Bible man or woman. The first one has been done for you.

1.

N	U	C
I	R	S
E	O	L

Cornelius

4.

S	A	M
EL	H	E
H	T	U

7.

E	R	A
S	S	U
H	U	A

2.

H	A	H
P	A	N
I	Z	E

5.

H	A	H
B	A	B
E	T	S

8.

E	E	E
L	C	L
H	I	M

3.

X	D	L
A	N	A
E	R	E

6.

TI	A	U
M	A	S
R	B	E

Answers are in the back of the book.

God's Promises - When You Lack Confidence

Cross out the words according to instructions given to reveal God's promise:

BE NINE HE I SILENT CAN LEFT HEAVEN DO END HERB FISH ALL HIS MOON ONE THINGS THOU THROUGH THREE SUN HIM EARTH CHRIST CREATURES TEN LIGHTS WHICH TIMES WATERS MY STRENGTHENETH BEHIND GRASS ME STARS NIGHT VISION.

1. Cross out masculine pronouns.
2. Cross out the name of a popular book series.
3. Cross out the subject of #2.
4. Cross out the name of a familiar hymn.
5. Cross out the name of a Christmas carol.
6. Cross out all numbers.
7. Cross out things mentioned in Genesis 1.

Answer is in the back of the book.

Words to Keep Close in Heart

Using the clues, locate each letter and put it on the line numbered as its clue. The result are words worth remembering.

```
A L M P S H O
E S I K O T Y
O N R S C G U
K A T O J E E
Q E G B A O I
N I C H D P T
U W E R O M L
```

1. This letter is in between a T and E.
2. This letter appears more often than any other letter.
3. This letter is in the sixth row, but no place else on the grid.
4. This letter is in the second and third columns.
5. This letter appears in row one.
6. This letter follows an O and M.
7. This letter is the same as the letter for clue 2.
8. This letter isn't on the grid.
9. This letter is one of the vowels in the last column.

___ ___ ___   ___ ___   ___ ___ ___ ___
1 2 3   4 5   6 7 8 9

Answers are in the back of the book.

Look Again!

There are 5 subtle differences between these two pictures. Can you find them?

...the greatest of these is love.

Bible Places Crossword

ACROSS

3 Where God sent Jonah
5 Fire and brimstone city
8 Jesus raised a widow's son here
10 Southern Kingdom
11 Site of Jesus' first miracle
12 Place where Paul lived under house arrest
13 Where Paul preached in the agora
16 Road to ___, where Jesus appeared after His resurrection
20 Its walls came tumbling down
21 Witch of ___
23 Plagues place
24 Tower of ___
26 Where Jesus healed the possessed man

DOWN

1 Jesus' birthplace
2 Dorcas' home
4 Where Jesus grew up
6 Mount of ___
7 City associated with Paul's conversion
9 Site of Jesus' crucifixion
10 Temple site
14 City of early Christian congregation
15 Garden where Jesus prayed
17 Ten Commandments mount
18 Mary and Martha's home
19 Abraham's birthplace
22 Land of milk and honey
25 First garden

Answers are in the back of the book.

Kids in the Bible

Kids play an important part in the history of God's people! Match the child with the event in which he or she played a part.

1. Boy with 5 loaves and 2 fish
2. A prostitute's infant
3. Jairus' daughter
4. Rhoda
5. Moses
6. Jesus
7. Nobleman's son
8. Samuel
9. Isaac

a. Raised from the dead by Jesus

b. Adopted by Pharaoh's daughter

c. Healed by Jesus from a distance

d. Entered temple service as a child

e. Feeding of the 5,000

f. Servant girl

g. Case showing Solomon's wisdom

h. Abraham's long-awaited son

i. Sat among scholars in the temple

Answers are in the back of the book.

Women Of The Bible Word Search

Mary	Anna	Martha	Huldah
Ruth	Dorcas	Miriam	Rachel
Hannah	Elizabeth	Judith	Naomi
Esther	Mary Magdalene	Tabitha	Priscilla
Deborah	Gomer	Dinah	Rebekah
Eve	Joanna	Orpah	
Sarah	Leah	Tamar	

```
O L H A N N A H G B U B H Y V R
P E W S X A D F H N A O M I F A
F R U T H T W N U U Y B I M O L
E V E A A U Y N L X R A C H E L
D V N O P I K L D T T G V N L I
Y I T M R D E S A A Q A E E I C
D V E A O N T B H T R L E S Z S
N T F R Y T I H J L A O M T A I
U Y C T V T X A D D N M M H B R
N A V H H E H R G E O H A E E P
S N E A Q T Z A G B L K I R T N
Y N T V I E M S Q O L O R I H U
H A Y T G Y T H R R M C I M O M
L O J H R F A N N A W E M T V A
E J R A T E H N I H M O R M I R
P L M B L T R E B E K A H C E Y
V R J U D I T H J Y N T G B I K
```

Answers are in the back of the book.

Relationships

Bible people had relatives–some of whom they got along with, others they didn't. Determine the relationships between these Bible pairs.

1. Moses was to Jethro as Ruth was to:
   a. Zipporah b. Orpah c. Naomi d. Mary
2. Leah was to Rachel as Martha was to:
   a. Mary b. Esther c. Sarah d. Joanna
3. Potiphar was to Joseph as Philemon was to:
   a. Pharaoh b. Onesimus c. David d. Silas
4. Timothy was to Lois as Jacob was to:
   a. Isaac b. Esau c. Nahor d. Abraham
5. Lazarus was to Mary as Aaron was to:
   a. Sarah b. Miriam c. Dorcas d. Deborah
6. Abraham was to Sarah as David was to:
   a. Jesse b. Tamar c. Michal d. Mary
7. Priscilla was to Aquila as Rebekah was to:
   a. Isaac b. Jacob c. Abraham d. Joseph

Answers are in the back of the book.

Day Job

Match the Bible name with his or her line of work!

Deborah	a. Shepherd
Paul	b. Tax Collector
Baruch	c. Fisher
Luke	d. Judge
Zacchaeus	e. Tailor
Lydia	f. Tentmaker
Andrew	g. Merchant
Amos	h. Scribe
Dorcas	i. Physician

Answers are in the back of the book.

Shared Letter

In each line of four Biblical names, there's one shared letter between all four names. Put the shared letter from each line on the blanks below to form another Biblical name.

1.	Absalom	Elisha	Saul	Esther
2.	David	Adam	Malachi	Mary
3.	Moses	Samson	Naomi	Martha
4.	Jesus	Jairus	Paul	Uriah
5.	Gideon	Gomer	Herodias	Hezekiah
6.	Jezebel	Israel	Silas	Elijah

Answer:

___ ___ ___ ___ ___ ___
1 2 3 4 5 6

Answers are in the back of the book.

Alpha and Omega

These Bible-connected words begin and end with the same letter. Use a different letter for each word.

Example: __ NN __ Anna

1. __ EN __
2. __ BB __
3. __ EA __
4. __ IRIA __
5. __ AI __
6. __ AVI __
7. __ AGL __
8. __ CACI __
9. __ IDO __
10. __ ULE __
11. __ EE __
12. __ IVE __

Answers are in the back of the book.

Bible Women Crossword

ACROSS

1 Early Christian teacher
5 Driven into the desert by 13 Across
6 Bore John, who became a Baptizer
10 Timothy's pious grandmother
13 Her name means "Princess"
15 First woman
17 Jacob's favored wife
19 She learned the secret of Samson's strength
20 Samuel's mom
23 Nabal's smart wife
24 Desert prophetess

DOWN

2 She stayed with 21 Down
3 Temple widow
4 Early Christian known for her needlework
7 Seller of purple cloth
8 Timothy's pious mother
9 Hosea's unfaithful wife
11 Solomon's mom
12 Sister of Lazarus
14 Wicked queen
16 Queen of Persia
18 She had 12 brothers
21 Orpah's mother-in-law
22 Magdalene

Answers are in the back of the book.

Look Again!

There are 5 subtle differences between these two pictures. Can you find them?

"Mom, I can't believe you really dressed that way when you were my age!"

Notable Events

Test your knowledge of Christian history by picking the correct definition of each:

1. The Crusades

a. Attempted conquest of the Holy Land during the 11th century.
b. Tent revival meetings throughout the U.S.
c. A series of best-selling Christian adventure stories.

2. The Diet of Worms

a. Title of a cookbook for unrepentant sinners.
b. Contentious religious debates of the 21st century.
c. Assembly in which Martin Luther was asked to recant his works.

3. The Sunday School Movement

a. Initially established to teach illiterate adults and children to read and write.
b. Initially established as a place to park the kids while parents went out for breakfast.
c. Initially established to supplement a church service.

4. Tyndale's Bible

a. First Latin Bible published.
b. First English Bible published.
c. First Gaelic Bible published.

5. The Jesus Movement

a. Crowds who followed Jesus during His ministry on earth.
b. All who believe the Good News of Jesus Christ.
c. Antiestablishment Christianity of the 1960s.

6. The Temperance Movement

a. Anti-alcohol.
b. Anti-anger.
c. Pro moderate temperatures.

Answers are in the back of the book.

Letter Mix

Cross out each letter from the alphabet list that you see in the box below. Rearrange the letters remaining in the alphabet list to form the name of one of Jesus' disciples.

A B C D E F G H I J K L M N O P Q R S T U V W X Y Z

C	V	S	H	L	P	G
B	U	I	Z	J	F	O
C	Q	G	V	Y	M	O
H	K	T	I	L	Q	U
K	X	Z	Y	S	M	Z
C	H	Q	K	O	U	P
S	Y	M	S	L	F	B
H	X	V	Z	K	M	C
I	P	I	F	G	L	Y
X	H	S	P	T		

Answer: ______________________

Answer is in the back of the book.

Look Again!

There are 5 subtle differences between these two pictures. Can you find them?

On the road of life, good friends are God's way of keeping us on the right path.

STOP
GR-8

God's Promise – When You're in Need

Find God's promise hidden in these words by following the instructions below:

1. Cross out all books of the Bible.
2. Cross out the name of a familiar hymn.
3. Cross out a saying by Benjamin Franklin.
4. Cross out the name of a biblical garden.
5. Cross out the names of various foods and herbs.

A LEAD PENNY ASK NUTS AND JONAH THOU SAVED

HOSEA YE ME IS BARLEY SHALL A RECEIVE FIGS

ON THAT EDEN BREAD PENNY ONIONS JOB YOUR

AMOS EGGS EARNED JOY MAY BE SALT MINT JOEL

BEANS FULL FISH.

Bible verse: ______________________________________

____

____

Answers are in the back of the book.

Lady, You're Under Arrest!

Identify the crime (or crimes) committed by these biblical women:

1. **LOT'S WIFE**
   a. Murder b. Disobedience c. Incest d. Sorcery

2. **POTIPHAR'S WIFE**
   a. Seduction b. Embezzlement c. False testimony
   d. Public intoxication

3. **DELILAH**
   a. Theft b. Murder c. Sorcery d. Betrayal

4. **JEZEBEL**
   a. Theft b. Idol worship c. Murder
   d. Child abandonment

5. **HERODIAS**
   a. Murder b. Lewd dancing c. Revenge
   d. Adultery

Answers are in the back of the book.

Words of a Feather

In each word-block below, there are three associated words, such as: APPLE, PEAR, APRICOT. Cross out the associated words. Write the first letter of each remaining word on the blanks below to spell out what Samuel said in answer to God's call.

SERMON SHEEP PATIENCE HYMN EWE ANNA KEEP PEW FULLNESS OMRI

REIGN THANK KING HONEST YEAST SAVE CROWN EZRA RACHEL THRONE

VINE LOVE ADORE NEEDS TEKOA JOY HALLELUJAH PEACE ESAU ABEL

WORDS RAMAH DEEDS EDOM TRINITY HOLY THOUGHTS

Bible verse: ___ ___ ___ ___ ___ ___ ___ ___

___ ___ ___ ___ ___ ___ ___ ___ ___ ___

___ ___ ___ ___ ___ ___ ___.

Answers are in the back of the book

Choices

Find answers by choosing one letter from each pair of letters, reading left to right.

Example: Eden was one

I**G** E**A** **R**C E**D** **E**T O**N**

1. A candle should not be covered with one
   BC EU VS OH EI LM

2. Bible bread ingredient
   WB AH RA LE TE TY

3. Ark measures
   MC UI LB IS GT MS

4. Moses parted it
   RM EA OD ST OE AY

5. Jesus rode one into Jerusalem
   SD OE NJ EK EI YN

6. House of worship
   CT AH UA OR CV EH

7. Day of worship for many
   TS EU ND ED IA YN

Answers are in the back of the book

Names of Jesus Crossword

The Bible and Christians refer to Jesus in many ways. Solve the clues below to fill in the crossword.

ACROSS

2 Prince of ___
5 Bread of ___
6 ___ and Omega (Rev. 1:8 kjv)
7 Messiah
11 ___ of Bethlehem
12 ___ of the World
15 "God with us"
16 ___ of David
17 Physician
18 ___ Child
20 Good ___

DOWN

1 ___ from on high (Luke 1:78 kjv)
3 Rabbi
4 Jesus ___
8 One who saves
9 "God of Israel"
10 Jesus of ___
12 The Word
13 "I am the way, the ___" (John 14:6 kjv)
14 ___ worker
19 ___ of God

Answers are in the back of the book.

Missing Pages

Every other letter has been omitted from these Books of the Bible. How quickly can you fill in the blanks?

___A___G___I

___H___L___M___N

___A___A___I___N___

___B___D___A___

___C___L___S___A___T___S

___E___R___W___

___H___L___P___I___N___

___A___A___K___K

___A___U___

___S___L___S

___I___O___H___

___O___O___S___A___S

Answers are in the back of the book.

Double Trouble Word Search

There are 23 Bible-related words, each containing a set of double letters. The first one is done for you.

Aaron
Accusers
Beersheba
Colossians
Deed
Ecclesiastes
Fulfillment
Good
Greed
Habakkuk
Haggai
Heed
Isaac
Keep
Look
Matthew
Seek
Sheep
Struggle
Suffer
Philippians
Weep

O O W L S O M E U M E L O O K S A W
I **S E E K** S A A R O N E N S U I G E
B R E E A S T C A O R N B E A D R S
C E P J T O T C L H A G G A I I E S
A A S P E N H E E D B E O O D E E D
V R A Y M T E Q U E S M P O R T D O
R A C L A I W R E S S O M M D R I M
E C C L E S I A S T E S E E T T L E
J E U V E A X T C O L O S S I A N S
S U S S E A I A R R N O T R P R I H
E T E R C C O H A B A K K U K E O E
S T R O O P B E E R S H E B A A N E
R E S U F F E R I C C A E P R M I P
P L U G G E P H I L I P P I A N S O
A I L A A G E W C O Z Z I L L E E D
F U L F I L L M E N T E P L L E E V
I U A F H E L E W E O D P A O T L O

Answers are in the back of the book.

Look Again!

There are 5 subtle differences between these two pictures. Can you find them?

"I've been thinking a lot about the hereafter, Pastor...More and more often, I find myself standing in a room thinking "Now what did I come in hereafter?"

Let's Eat!

In the puzzle, circle the Bible foods listed in the word box. Words may read forward, backward, up, down, or diagonally. The letters remaining, in order, spell part of a common table prayer!

ANISE	CORN
MINT	FISH
SALT	WHEAT
BEANS	HONEY
BARLEY	EGGS
MUSTARD	MILK
LEEKS	WINE
FIGS	LAMB
NUTS	RUE
OLIVES	RYE

E	N	I	W	F	L	A	M	B
L	S	E	V	I	L	O	E	D
T	A	T	H	S	E	S	R	M
L	E	N	G	H	I	A	F	I
E	R	M	I	N	T	T	S	L
E	U	T	O	S	U	B	S	K
K	E	B	U	B	E	A	N	S
S	E	M	E	N	B	R	Y	E
L	G	E	S	U	T	L	A	S
S	G	I	E	T	A	E	H	W
D	S	A	F	S	M	Y	E	N
C	O	R	N	Y	E	N	O	H

Answer:

____

____

____

____

____

Church Meeting

Enter the names of everyone who attended the church meeting. The first name has been entered for you. (Anyone think to ask the Lord to come?)

3 Letters	4 Letters	5 Letters
Asa	Abel	Aaron
Dan	Adam	Abram
Eve	Amos	David
Ham	Anna	Hosea
Job	Cain	Jacob
	Esau	James
	John	Jesse
	Levi	Moses
	Lois	Peter
	Luke	Rhoda
	Mark	Rufus
	Noah	Simon

Answers are in the back of the book.

E
V
E

Look Again!

There are 5 subtle differences between these two pictures. Can you find them?

O Come Let Us Adore Him

Parables Of Jesus Word Search

Lamp Under A Basket
The Sower
The Weeds
Mustard Seed
Hidden Treasure
Lost Sheep
Wedding Feast
Fig Tree
Good Samaritan
Wise Man's Foundation
Prodigal Son
Rich Man And Lazarus

L	W	E	D	D	I	N	G	F	E	A	S	T	M	I	T
N	W	E	W	S	E	D	C	U	K	O	H	H	G	E	N
H	I	E	S	Q	X	E	P	O	M	L	K	E	K	U	N
Y	S	D	E	E	W	E	H	T	A	L	O	S	I	N	S
H	E	Y	T	G	V	R	F	R	E	D	A	O	M	O	U
L	M	J	H	G	F	T	S	A	Q	B	E	W	T	V	R
E	A	U	D	T	Y	G	N	I	A	M	O	E	M	I	A
P	N	O	S	G	T	I	F	R	C	W	S	R	C	E	Z
V	S	F	B	T	T	F	E	J	Y	N	T	G	B	I	A
O	F	P	K	I	A	D	P	E	E	H	S	T	S	O	L
P	O	W	S	X	N	R	F	A	K	D	P	F	M	N	D
F	U	N	U	U	T	W	D	O	U	Y	B	I	M	O	N
Y	N	V	P	O	U	Y	N	S	X	A	F	M	N	S	A
D	D	M	O	M	I	K	L	P	E	T	G	V	N	L	N
Y	A	T	F	R	D	E	S	W	A	E	A	M	H	A	A
L	T	E	D	U	N	T	C	R	V	R	D	E	I	G	M
N	I	E	R	U	S	A	E	R	T	N	E	D	D	I	H
G	O	O	D	S	A	M	A	R	I	T	A	N	B	D	C
O	N	P	K	I	M	Y	N	G	B	U	B	H	Y	O	I
W	E	W	S	X	A	D	F	A	K	D	P	F	M	R	R
F	E	N	U	G	T	W	N	O	U	Y	B	I	M	P	L

Answers are in the back of the book.

God's Promise When You Pray

Follow the directions to reveal God's promise to you when you pray to Him.

1. In even-numbered lines, cross out books of the Bible.
2. In line 3, cross out two repeated words.
3. In odd-numbered lines, cross out rhyming words.
4. Cross out the name of a Christmas carol hidden in one of the lines.
5. In lines 2 and 3, cross out words related to gardening.
6. In line 1, cross out words ending in d.
7. In line 5, cross out words ending in l.
8. In lines 1, 4 and 5, cross out desk items.

1. the ruler Lord eyes land night pen of the lifted light lied
2. plant acts Lord reap are kings flower upon hoe judges the
3. soil the righteous seed star sow and his plant the far fruit
4. ears oh job are mouse mark come open all ye faithful
5. all unto soul clip seed their eternal paper deed real cry

____

____

Answers are in the back of the book.

Animals Of The Bible Word Search

adder	goat	camel	flea
asp	owl	sparrow	lamb
bear	ox	swallow	leopard
bee beetle	hen	donkey	lion
behemoth	heron	dove	locust
bird	ram	turtle dove	whale
boar	raven	eagle	wolf
gnat	calf	fish	

```
N T F B Y T G H J T A N G U I O
A D D E R E X W D Y N O L M D J
N Y V A S A D L M K E H B G R N
H F D R I B O P O L L A I J A N
Y B T V F C X B T A L O G I P U
H B Y L U G N E T H S I F L O P
L S O S G F E S A E W E O T E R
E W T N T B S P A R R O W N L T
F A N U E T E N O O Y B I M O U
F L V E O V L H E N A F M N V R
D L B O M I A L E L T L T N B T
Y O E L R D H R A M Q A M H I L
R W E A U N W C R V O C T M E E
P L O M G T Y F E G W T X C E D
V R F B G T M U V Y L T H B I O
O L P K Y E K N O D U B P S A V
P C A M E L D F D K D P F M I E
```

Answers are in the back of the book.

Tour of the Holy Land

Pastor Smith is leading a tour of the Holy Land, and these are the places he plans to visit:

BETHLEHEM	GALILEE
CAESAREA	GETHSEMANE
CANA	JERICHO
CAPERNAUM	JERUSALEM
EMMAUS	NAZARETH

Help him with his itinerary by locating all ten places in the chart below by linking adjoining circles. Circles may be joined up, down, forward, backward, or diagonally. Not all circles will be used. **EMMAUS** is done for you...

GE	CA	ES	OL	CE	JE	AM
PER	EE	MO	AR	RU	LO	RIC
NA	ZA	LUL	GET	EA	SAL	HO
UM	AU	RE	CA	HS	MN	EM
GA	BE	TH	LEH	EM	ANE	ZE
LIL	NA	CA	**EM** →	**MA** ↙	NE	MM
OM	EE	RU	**US**	LI	HO	MN

Answers are in the back of the book.

Match Ups

See if you can match each name in the first column with a related word in the second column.

BIBLE PLACES

1. One of the 7 churches in Revelation	a. Sinai
2. City defeated by Joshua	b. Smyrna
3. 10 Commandments site	c. Damascus
4. City where Jonah preached	d. Jerusalem
5. Site of Jacob's Ladder dream	e. Tekoa
6. City of David	f. Capernaum
7. Home of Amos the prophet	g. Jericho
8. Jesus visited here many times	h. Nineveh
9. Paul led here after his conversion	i. Bethel

BIBLE PEOPLE

1. Oldest person
2. Wicked king
3. Good queen
4. Giant
5. Leader out of Egypt
6. Priest
7. Forerunner of Jesus
8. Mother of 6 sons
9. Raised by Peter from the dead

a. Moses
b. Leah
c. John the Baptist
d. Eli
e. Ahab
f. Dorcas
g. Methuselah
h. Goliath
i. Esther

Answers are in the back of the book.

Look Again!

There are 5 subtle differences between these two pictures. Can you find them?

"He's Got the Whole World in His Hands"

Front-Word, Back-Word

The clue in the first column is a word that, read backward, answers the clue in the second column.

Clue	Answer	Clue
1. Magi followed it	____________	An exclamation
2. Morning moisture	____________	Like Abraham and Sarah, for example
3. Hold on to	____________	Sneaked glimpse
4. Commandment number	____________	Fisherman's need
5. Poet	____________	Dull
6. Jesus' cross	____________	Entrance
7. Stairway feature	____________	Dogs and cats, often
8. Fierce battle	____________	Not cooked
9. Pen tip	____________	Container
10. Circle	____________	Bethesda was one
11. Doze	____________	Strips
12. Jonathan to David, for example	____________	Swimmer's distance
13. Insane	____________	Reservoir sight
14. The best!	____________	Stain

Answers are in the back of the book.

Evening Star

See how many 4-letter words you can form by moving from one letter to the next along lines. You can go in any direction the lines go, and you can return to a letter. However, do not skip letters or count a letter twice by staying on it. No plurals!

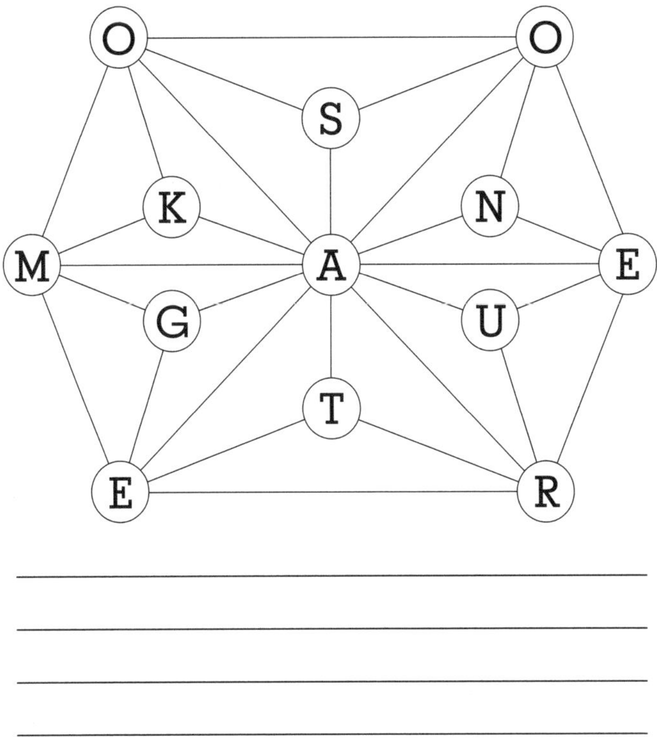

Answers are in the back of the book.

Creation Sings

The Psalmist wrote songs and poems of thanks and praise to God for the majesty of creation. Selecting from the word box below, fill in the blanks with the natural wonder mentioned by the Psalmist.

MOUNTAINS	STARS
TREE	EARTH
SKIES	SUN
FIELD	HEAVEN
EARTH	TREES
EARTH	HILLS
CLOUDS	MOON
HEAVENS	RIVERS
WOOD	SEA
MOON	EARTH
SEAS	

1. When I consider thy ________, the work of thy fingers, the ________ and the ________, which thou has ordained (Psalm 8:3).

2. Let all the ________ fear the LORD (Psalm 33:8).

3. And he shall be like a ________ planted by the ________ of water (Psalm 1:3).

4. He appointed the ________ for seasons; the ________ knoweth his going down (Psalm 104:19).

5. Let the ________ and ________ praise him, the ________, and every thing that moveth therein (Psalm 69:34).

6. Therefore will not we fear, though the ________ be removed, and though the ________ be carried into the midst of the ________ (Psalm 46:2).

7. In his hand are the deep places of the ________: the strength of the ________ is his also (Psalm 95:4).

8. The ________ poured out water: the ________ sent out a sound: thine arrows also went abroad (Psalm 77:17).

9. Let the ________ be joyful, and all that is therein: then shall all the ________ of the ________ rejoice (Psalm 96:12).

Answers are in the back of the book.

Double Meaning

Many words are spelled the same but have different meanings. Write the word that fits both phrases of each quote. When you are finished, the first letter of each word will spell the name of a popular and much-loved saint.

1. "I didn't feel this way...after paying the consequence for my speeding ticket."
2. "I'll take my ease...for the remainder of the day."
3. "I'll talk to the crowd...from my own front porch."
4. "Be civil...when you visit this French city."
5. "The entire acting company...wore one after they broke a leg."
6. "Let's talk about the problem...with this magazine."
7. "I'd like to be a stitcher...but the plumber's here to unclog the drains."

1. ☐ ______
2. ☐ ______
3. ☐ ______
4. ☐ ______
5. ☐ ______
6. ☐ ______
7. ☐ ______

Answers are in the back of the book.

Places Of The Bible Word Search

Antioch	Damascus	Nazareth
Bethlehem	Emmaus	Tarsus
Caesarea	Ephesus	Tyre
Cana	Joppa	
Capernaum	Jericho	
Corinth	Jerusalem	

```
O L P K I E Y N G B U B H Y V R
P J W S X A M F A K D P F M I P
F E N U G T W M O T A R S U S L
Y R C A P E R N A U M F M N N C
D U W N M I K L P U A G V N A A
Y S T T R D E P H A S U S H Z P
R A E I U N T C R V C D E S A P
N L F O B T G H J L U O M U R O
U E H C V E X H D E S O L M E J
N M V H S E T C U K R H B G T N
H F E S Q N Z H O M L I I J H N
Y B T V I E S W L A L O C I N U
H B Y R G V A F T E D C I H O P
L K O H G F N S Y Q H E R T O R
E C R D T Y A E R A S E A C I K
P L O B G T C F E C W S M C E D
V R F B G T M U J Y N T G B I K
```

Answers are in the back of the book.

Who? What? When? Where?

Choose the correct answer to these Bible questions!

1. **What were the Israelites doing when Moses came down from Mount Sinai?**
   a. Praising God b. Worshiping a golden calf
   c. Waiting patiently

2. **Where was Paul when he experienced conversion?**
   a. On the road to Damascus b. At home c. In the temple

3. **Why did women go out to Jesus' tomb early Sunday morning?**
   a. To plant flowers b. To visit one another c. To anoint His body

4. **Who is the main author of Psalms?**
   a. Solomon b. David c. Saul

5. **Who told Mary she would have a child?**
   a. A prophet b. Her physician c. An angel

6. **What was the reason Mary and Joseph fled with their baby to Egypt?**
   a. King Herod's murderous reign b. The magi told them to
   c. Their in-laws

7. **Where did John the Baptizer baptize people?**
   a. Pool of Bethesda b. Sea of Galilee c. Jordan River

8. **Which of the 12 tribes of Israel was the priestly tribe?**
   a. Dan   b. Asher   c. Levi

9. **Who is called the "weeping prophet"?**
   a. Jeremiah   b. Joshua   c. Joel

10. **What happened to Adam and Eve after the Fall?**
    a. They stayed in the Garden of Eden
    b. They were sent away from Eden   c. They fled to Egypt

11. **Who are the two Old Testament figures taken by God directly to heaven?**
    a. Eve and Ezra   b. Enoch and Elijah   c. Elisha and Eleazar

12. **Where did the writing on the wall take place?**
    a. Jerusalem   b. Damascus   c. Babylon

13. **What happened to Samson after he was captured?**
    a. He was blinded   b. He was flogged then freed
    c. He was sent home

14. **Why was Jonah swallowed by a fish?**
    a. It was an accident   b. He had tried to avoid God's command
    c. The fish was hungry

Answers are in the back of the book.

Echoes of the Bible

Many quotes and phrases commonly used today in conversation and in literature are from the Bible. How many can you identify? Name the speaker or writer; and context.

1. "The greatest of these is love."

___

2. "Am I my brother's keeper?"

___

3. "The Lord is my shepherd."

___

4. "Behold the man!"

___

5. "Let my people go!"

___

6. "Blessed art thou among women."

___

7. "Whither thou goest, I will go."

____

8. "Do you betray the Son of Man with a kiss?"

____

9. "How do you know you aren't here for such a time as this?"

____

10. "You are bone of my bones, flesh of my flesh."

____

11. "How can I do this great wickedness and sin against God?"

____

12. "Feed my sheep."

____

Answers are in the back of the book.

God's Faithfulness

A Bible truth about God's faithfulness can be found from "Let us" by moving from adjoining boxes in any direction, including diagonally.

PROFESSION	THE	FAITH	WITHOUT
OF	OUR	FAST	WAVERING
LET US	HOLD	HE	FOR
PROMISED	THAT	FAITHFUL	IS

Let us ________________________________

____

____

____

____

Answers are in the back of the book.

An Eventful Journey

Moses led the Children of Israel from Egypt and to the Promised Land. During their 40 years' wandering and before they reached their destination, a lot happened! Put these 12 events in order as they took place in the Bible account:

__ Out of anger, Moses breaks the two tablets of stone given to Him by God. (Exodus 32:19-20)

__ Joshua leads the Israelites across the Jordan River. (Joshua 3:14-17)

__ Aaron makes a golden calf for the people to worship. (Exodus 32:1-4)

__ God sends manna and quail for His people to eat. (Exodus 16:13-15)

__ Joshua sends spies into Canaan. (Joshua 2:1)

__ Moses receives the Commandments a second time. (Exodus 34:28)

__ The Israelites build a tabernacle. (Exodus 39:32)

__ The Israelites celebrate the first Passover. (Exodus 12:1-28)

__ Moses dies. (Deuteronomy 34:5)

__ The Israelites cross the Red Sea on dry land. (Exodus 14:21-22)

__ After 430 years in Egypt, the Israelites depart. (Exodus 12:40-41)

__ Moses receives the Ten Commandments from God. (Exodus 20:1-17)

Answers are in the back of the book.

Stop and Smell the Roses

"He hath made everything beautiful in His time."
Ecclesiastes 3:11

The gardener planted all kinds of flowers in her garden, but she forgot to weed. Can you find the 21 flowers she planted?

```
T O S N A P D R A G O N I N G
B E A M S Z D A F F O D I L I
U M Z S E N E S L I L U R S N
T E A U T I V A I N E D R A G
T N L M O E O I V I O L E T S
A R E C Q U R L P O R D S I S
O C A R N A T I O N H A I A W
N P W I T I N G S I R I S E E
P E T L L I L Y E M I S P I E
A T U M I N S P A N S Y E U T
Z U L I A L U M S O E S O N P
I N I A S O A L I R I N N S E
R I P E N S Y C P O P P Y P A
M A R I G O L D C S I C O R I
U C Z I N N I A M E N O S I S
M A M S S T E N N O B E U L B
```

Answers are in the back of the book.

Bible Connections

Draw a line from the Bible name to his or her Bible connection!

1. Moses	a. Locusts and wild honey
2. Aaron	b. Valley of dry bones
3. John the Baptist	c. Fiery furnace
4. Lot's wife	d. Devastating loss
5. Judas Iscariot	e. Burning bush
6. Ezekiel	f. Handwriting on the wall
7. Daniel	g. Budding staff
8. Shadrach, Meshach, Abednego	h. Lion's den
9. Belshazzar	i. Pillar of salt
10. Job	j. 30 pieces of silver

Answers are in the back of the book.

Scripture Match Up

Can you match the reference with the phrase or verse?

1. Continue in prayer, and watch in the same with thanksgiving	Numbers 6:24
2. Trust in the Lord with all thine heart and lean not unto thine own understanding	Proverbs 1:5
3. Come unto me all ye that labour and are heavy laden, and I will give you rest	Colossians 4:2
4. A wise man will hear, and will increase learning; and a man of understanding shall attain unto wise counsels	Psalm 27:14
5. Wait on the Lord; be of good courage, and He shall strengthen thine heart	Proverbs 3:5
6. I am the bread of life..he that cometh to me shall never hunger and he that believeth on me shall never thirst	John 6:35
7. The Lord bless thee, and keep thee	Matthew 11:28

Answers are in the back of the book.

Word Shuffle

From the word list below, select three words that fit into each category. Many words fit in more than one category, but only one arrangement will provide three words for each category. Use each word only once.

ROMANS	SAMUEL	RUTH	MELCHIZEDEK	ESTHER	JUDGES
MATTHEW	EZEKIEL	ELIZABETH	GENESIS	ORPAH	ELIJAH
GALILEE	AHAB	LUKE	NATHANAEL	MARY	GALATIANS
JUDAH	ELI	JOSEPH	ANDREW	REBEKAH	JOHN
CORINTHIANS	GILGAL	HEROD	ANNA	LEAH	PAUL
AMOS	PETER	PSALMS	DANIEL	DAVID	NAOMI

1. Jesus' disciples ________ ________ ________
2. Priests ________ ________ ________
3. Places ________ ________ ________
4. O.T. books ________ ________ ________
5. Epistles ________ ________ ________
6. Brides ________ ________ ________
7. Gospel books ________ ________ ________
8. Mothers ________ ________ ________
9. Kings ________ ________ ________
10. Prophets ________ ________ ________
11. Widows ________ ________ ________
12. Prisoners ________ ________ ________

Answers are in the back of the book.

Word Search

The words in the list below are associated with a familiar parable. Words may read forward, backward, up, down, or diagonally. When you have found all the words in the word search puzzle (next page), the remaining letters will spell out an appropriate title for the parable.

Word List

ALIVE	PIGS	SINS
CALF	RAN	SIRE
FEAST	RING	SKID
FOUND	ROBE	SORRY
GAVE	SAD	STY
ILL	SAY	TWO
IRE	SEAMY	YES
KISS	SERVANT	

G	N	I	R	R	T	W	O
P	S	E	R	V	A	N	T
S	R	S	F	S	I	N	S
A	I	O	S	E	A	M	Y
Y	L	N	D	G	A	V	E
F	L	A	C	I	I	S	S
A	L	I	V	E	G	P	T
F	L	S	K	I	D	A	Y
O	O	I	I	S	A	D	L
U	Y	R	S	O	R	R	Y
N	A	E	S	R	O	B	E
D	L	F	A	T	H	E	R

Parable Title: ______________________________

Answers are in the back of the book.

Bible Crossword

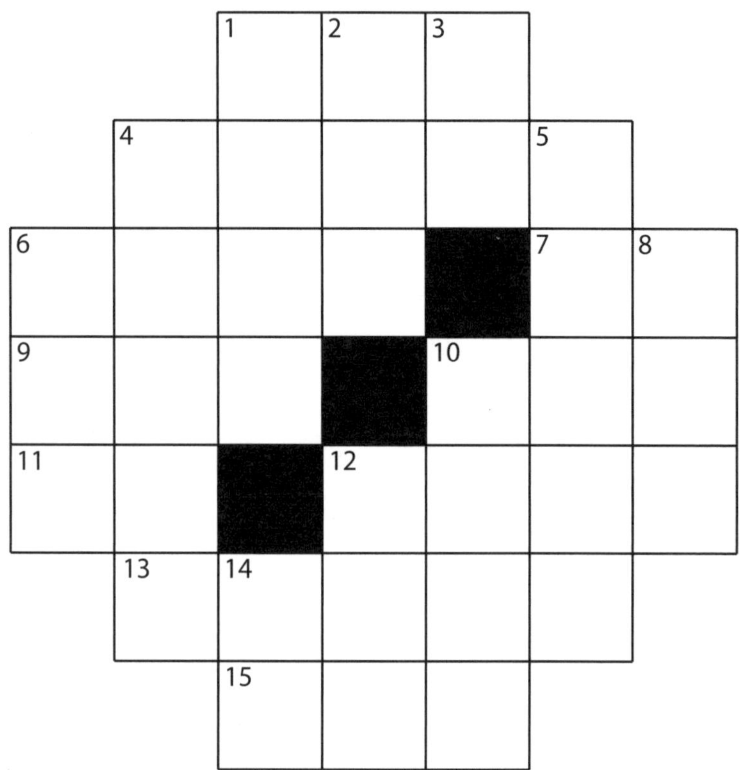

Across

1. "I once was blind, but now I ___"
4. O.T. false gods
6. Gasp for air
7. Classroom helper (Abbr.)
9. Isaac's dad, familiarly
10. Jacob's seventh son
11. "Jesus Loves __"
12. Sacred gemstones
13. Of the moon
15. "Thy ___ and thy staff they comfort me" (Ps. 23:4 KJV)

Down

1. Reasonable
2. "We remember the fish, which we did ___ in Egypt" (Num. 11:5 KJV)
3. ___-Shaddai, "God Almighty"
4. O.T. tower
5. Set of steps
6. Cooking spray
8. Org. department
10. One who completed high school (abbrev.)
12. Card game
14. Native place to 9 Across

Answers are in the back of the book.

Bible Stars

The letters of three names from the Bible - Dorcas, Mark, Eli-have been dropped into circles inside the star. How many four-letter words can you form by moving along the lines from circle to circle? You cannot skip a letter or count a letter twice, but you can go back to a letter. No capitalized words or plurals allowed. We found 22 words.

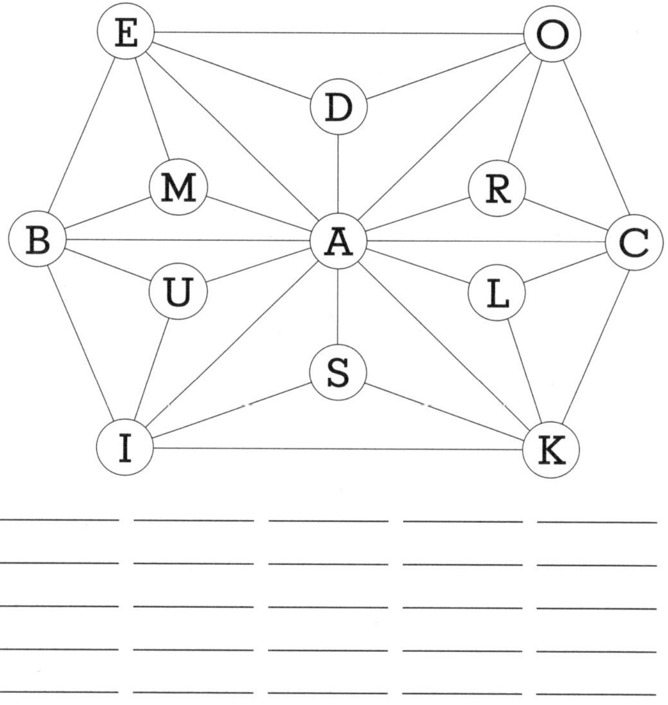

______ ______ ______ ______ ______

______ ______ ______ ______ ______

______ ______ ______ ______ ______

______ ______ ______ ______ ______

______ ______ ______ ______ ______

Answers are in the back of the book.

Comparisons

The first part of each statement refers to a certain relationship. To complete the second part, pick the word that follows the same relationship.

Example: Cain is to Abel as Peter is to Andrew
(two sets of brothers)

1. David is to king as Felix is to ________________.
   a. dictator b. governor c. prince d. servant

2. Peter is to fisherman as Paul is to ________________.
   a. tent maker b. carpenter c. cook d. tax collector

3. Genesis is to Moses as Acts is to ________________.
   a. Paul b. Silas c. Mark d. Luke

4. Noah is to flood as Shadrach, Meshach and Abednego are to

   ________________.

   a. lion's den b. big fish c. fiery furnace d. herbs & spices

5. Elisha is to Elijah as Timothy is to ________________.
   a. Paul b. Apollos c. Stephen d. Titus

6. Denial is to Peter as doubt is to ________________.
   a. Mark b. Matthew c. Thomas d. Bartholomew

7. Healing is to miracle as sower is to ________________.
   a. proverb b. parable c. sermon d. hymn

8. Tree of Life is to Eden as temple is to ________________.
   a. Jerusalem b. synagogue c. church d. Judah

Answers are in the back of the book.

What Is It?

Pick the right description for each named object.

1. BABEL
a. Mountain
b. Tower
c. Altar

2. EDEN
a. Garden
b. Tree
c. Serpent

3. GOLGOTHA
a. River
b. Hill
c. Town

4. EBENEZER
a. Stone
b. Tree
c. River

5. JORDAN
a. Sea
b. Pond
c. River

6. EPHOD
a. Rod
b. Temple
c. Garment

7. GALILEE
a. Garden
b. Lake
c. Pasture

8. ADAR
a. Month
b. Year
c. Day

9. PRAETORIUM
a. Arena
b. Hall
c. Roof

10. BAAL
a. Haystack
b. Cart
c. Idol

Answers are in the back of the book.

Parents and Children

Match each Bible child with his or her mother!

1. DINAH
a. Rachel
b. Leah
c. Sarah

2. SOLOMON
a. Bathsheba
b. Elizabeth
c. Delilah

3. MIRIAM
a. Rachel
b. Joanna
c. Jochebed

4. OBED
a. Esther
b. Ruth
c. Naomi

5. SETH
a. Eve
b. Sarah
c. Rebekah

6. SAMUEL
a. Mary
b. Hannah
c. Ruth

7. TIMOTHY
a. Lois
b. Eunice
c. Dorcas

8. JAMES
a. Sarah
b. Joanna
c. Mary

9. JESUS
a. Mary
b. Sarah
c. Rebekah

Answers are in the back of the book.

Famous Words

Pick the speaker of each Bible quote!

1. "Am I my brother's keeper?"
   a. Abel b. Noah c. Cain
2. "Thou shalt love thy neighbor as thyself."
   a. Jesus b. Luke c. Mark
3. "Behold the man!"
   a. Ananias b. Pilate c. Herod
4. "Behold the handmaid of the Lord; be it unto me according to thy word."
   a. Mary b. Dorcas c. Sarah
5. "Blessed are the peacemakers: for they shall be called the children of God."
   a. Paul b. John c. Jesus
6. "Silver and gold have I none; but such as I have give I thee."
   a. Jesus b. Peter c. John
7. "If I perish, I perish."
   a. Delilah b. Deborah c. Esther

Answers are in the back of the book.

Timeless Truth

Cross off the words below according to the directions. The remaining words will form a quote from the book of Proverbs.

STIR	MADE	A	PEAR
REVELATION	WADE	SOFT	NUMBERS
APRICOT	LAID	ANSWER	SCREEN
SIFT	JOEL	PINEAPPLE	RUTH
MOUSE	TURNS	POMEGRANATE	JUDGES
MARK	PEACH	BANANA	AWAY
PRINT	FADE	MODEM	EXODUS
JUDE	BLEND	BYTE	RAID
ACTS	WRATH	SURF	BAKE
BERRY	BROWSE		

Eliminate -

- kinds of fruit
- five words that rhyme
- cooking terms
- names of Bible books
- words associated with computers

____

Answers are in the back of the book.

Who said it?

Match the rhyme with the speaker, using the list of names in the box below:

PAUL	PETER	MARTHA
ANNA	SARAH	DAVID
SIMEON	RUTH	NOAH

A. I swore I'd be loyal no matter what came—
But instead I denied Him, and felt bitter shame.

____

B. As Abraham's wife and late in my life,
I held my first son at ninety and one!

____

C. In the temple we saw Him—our Messiah and Lord!
He was born as God promised and prophets foretold!

____

D. I slew a tough giant with a stone and a sling,
And was later anointed as Israel's king.

____

E. Of resurrected Jesus, I would have no part
Until the Holy Spirit changed my hardened heart.

____

F. I'm glad I obeyed–though far from the sea,
The ark that I built saved my family and me!

____

G. I stayed with Naomi and went to her land,
Then soon Boaz saw me and asked for my hand.

____

H. My sister sat by Him and listened
instead of helping me serve food–
The Lord said I was way too busy,
and Mary chose the greater good.

____

Answers are in the back of the book.

Bible Crossword Puzzle

			1	2	3			
			4					
			5					
6	7	8		■	9	10	11	12
13			■	■	■	14		
15			16	■	17			
			18	19				
			20					
			21					

ACROSS

1. Hannah's priest (1 Sam. 1:9)
4. Luke was one, for short (Col. 4:14)
5. Deer relative
6. Cut of meat
9. Thread from Egypt (2 Chr. 1:16)
13. There was no room in one (Luke 2:7)
14. Bring legal action against
15. Ruth's husband (Ruth 4:13)
17. Rave's partner
18. Adam's partner (Gen. 3:20)
20. Swift deer (Prov. 6:5)
21. Night hooter

DOWN

1. Residence of 18 Across (Gen. 2:8)
2. E-mail acronym
3. Describes day-old manna (Exo. 16:20)
6. Women's ___, feminist movement
7. Town built by the sons of Elpaal (1 Chr. 8:12)
8. "Lead me __ __ plain path" (Psa. 27:11)
10. King of Judah (1 King 15:8)
11. What you should do from temptation
12. Peter cast it into the sea (Matt. 4:18)
16. Number before one
17. Holds fishing line
19. Solemn promise

Answers are in the back of the book.

Find the Books

There are 20 books of the Bible hidden in the box below. They may be written left-to-right; right to left; vertically; or diagonally. Many overlap. Can you find them all?

Amos	Kings	Acts	Job
Mark	Hosea	Jonah	Luke
Ezra	Nahum	Malachi	Peter
Joel	Daniel	Esther	Psalms
Titus	Romans	Jeremiah	John

E	N	O	K	R	A	M	O	S	O	L	I
I	Z	A	H	O	S	A	R	O	J	V	A
T	O	R	D	M	A	L	E	J	O	E	L
I	O	N	A	A	V	A	H	E	B	U	P
T	I	A	N	N	J	C	T	R	K	J	E
U	T	H	I	S	O	H	S	E	C	U	T
S	H	U	E	U	N	I	E	M	L	D	E
G	O	M	L	B	A	K	N	I	H	E	R
N	S	N	A	E	H	P	S	A	L	M	S
I	E	O	G	A	I	E	U	H	K	A	M
K	A	C	T	S	W	O	W	J	O	H	N
S	A	V	I	O	R	A	H	S	A	L	M

Answers are in the back of the book.

Common Threads

The words in each group have something in common. What is it?

1. Simon, Philip, Andrew
   a. tribes of Israel
   b. apostles
   c. kings

2. Genesis, Exodus, Leviticus
   a. Pentateuch
   b. Gospels
   c. Epistles

3. Amos, Micah, Hosea
   a. disciples
   b. rulers
   c. prophets

4. Gethsemane, Eden, Resurrection
   a. cities
   b. streets
   c. gardens

5. Asa, Hezekiah, Josiah
   a. missionaries
   b. kings
   c. prophets

6. Joppa, Gibeon, Haran
   a. cities
   b. generals
   c. tribes

Answers are in the back of the book.

Bible Connections

Pick the matching relationship in each statement.

1. Miriam is to Moses as Martha is to ________.

   a. Mary b. Jesus c. Lazarus d. Anna

2. David is to king as Felix is to ________.

   a. governor b. prince c. mayor d. high priest

3. Ananias is to Sapphira as Aquila is to ________.

   a. Dorcas b. Phoebe c. Priscilla d. Apollos

4. Joppa is to Dorcas as Bethany is to ________.

   a. Joanne b. Mary c. Bernice d. Eve

5. Messiah is to Jesus as Baptizer is to ________.

   a. Micah b. Joseph c. Peter d. John

6. Eve is to fruit as Jonah is to ________.

a. ark b. chariot c. water d. fish

7. Peter is to fish as Matthew is to ________.

a. sheep b. taxes c. wine d. dry goods

8. Abraham is to Isaac as Jesse is to ________.

a. David b. Cain c. Daniel d. Benjamin

9. The Epistle to the Corinthians is to Paul as the book of Acts is to ________.

a. John b. Baruch c. Luke d. Peter

10. Saul is to Paul as Jacob is to ________.

a. Judah b. Israel c. Abraham d. Solomon

Answers are in the back of the book.

Bible Events

Match the Bible event with the name or names most closely identified with it.

The Flood	a. Jesus
Pentecost	b. Moses
The Fall	c. Noah
Sermon on the Mount	d. Joshua
Destruction of Sodom	e. Adam and Eve
Exodus from Egypt	f. Lot
Battle of Jericho	g. Peter

Answers are in the back of the book.

Books of the Bible

In each set of words, one "book" is not in the Bible. Can you identify it? Circle your answers.

1. Judges, Ruth, Samson, Genesis, Amos
2. Paul, Mark, Peter, Matthew, James
3. Isaiah, Ezra, Baruch, Nahum, Zephaniah
4. Deuteronomy, Leviticus, Numbers, Covenant, Psalms
5. Ephesians, Israel, Hebrews, Colossians, Philippians
6. Haggai, Hosea, Ezekiel, Adar, Joel
7. Joseph, Titus, Luke, John, Philemon
8. Galatians, Malachi, Hezekiah, Daniel, Obadiah
9. Micah, Andrew, Acts, Jude, Esther

Answers are in the back of the book.

Who Said It Where?

"What" is given to you, but you need to pick "Who?" and "Where?" for each action!

1. "I hid two spies from Israel," said ___,

   a. Martha b. Jezebel c. Rahab

   ...when I was living in ___."

   a. Jerusalem b. Jericho c. Sodom

2. "My brothers sold me to a troupe of traveling Midianites," said ___,

   a. Reuben b. Jesse c. Joseph

   ...and that's how I ended up in ___."

   a. Egypt b. Canaan c. Lebanon

3. "A big fish prepared by the Lord swallowed me," said ___,

   a. Joseph b. Jonah c. John

   ...and I soon found myself delivered to ___."

   a. Damascus b. Nazareth c. Nineveh

4. "I was blinded by a great light," said ___,

   a. Timothy b. Paul c. Silas

   ...and I was led to the city of ___."

   a. Damascus b. Nazareth c. Ninevah

5. "I demanded to have my case heard by Caesar," said ___,

   a. Paul b. Peter c. Silas

   ...and so soldiers took me to ___."

   a. Caesarea b. Athens c. Rome

Answers are in the back of the book.

Notable Women

Match the woman's Biblical "claim to fame" with her name!

1. She was a judge in Old Testament Israel.
   a. Deborah b. Rebekah c. Miriam

2. Her devoted daughter-in-law, Ruth, would not leave her.
   a. Mary b. Naomi c. Orpah

3. She risked her life to speak to the king on behalf of her people.
   a. Esther b. Vashti c. Miriam

4. She laughed when she heard she was to bear a son at her advanced age.
   a. Mary b. Hannah c. Sarah

5. She was in the Temple when Joseph and Mary brought in the Baby Jesus.
   a. Anna b. Elizabeth c. Martha

6. She and her husband, Aquila, were teachers in the early church.
   a. Dorcas b. Priscilla c. Bernice

7. She was among the women at the open tomb on the morning of Christ's resurrection.
   a. Phoebe b. Leah c. Joanna

Answers are in the back of the book.

Notable Men

Match the man's Biblical "claim to fame" with his name!

1. He parted the Red Sea.

   a. Aaron b. Moses c. Pharaoh

2. He was anointed Israel's first king.

   a. Paul b. David c. Saul

3. Samuel served under him in the Temple.

   a. Eli b. Elisha c. Elija

4. He was the first Christian stoned to death because of his faith.

   a. Paul b. Stephen c. Timothy

5. He was exiled to the Isle of Patmos.

   a. Matthew b. Mark c. John

6. He climbed up a sycamore tree so he could see Jesus as He passed by.

   a. Bartholomew b. Zacchaeus c. Titus

7. He needed to see with his own eyes that Jesus had risen from the dead.

   a. John b. Luke c. Thomas

Answers are in the back of the book.

It's Heavenly!

How many words of three letters or more can you form from the word HEAVENLY? You can use each letter only as many times as it appears in HEAVENLY. No words beginning with capital letters allowed. We found 21!

H E A V E N L Y

Answers are in the back of the book.

Bible Combos

Combine letter groups from columns 1, 2 and 3 (in that order) to form books of the Bible. Each group will be used only once. The first one has been done for you.

1	2	3
SA	ADI	UA
CO	OVE	ON
TI	CHAR	EL
OB	GG	WS
CHR	MU	RBS
JO	LATI	HY
PR	TH	CLES
PHI	BRE	IAH
HA	MOT	AI
GA	LEM	ER
HE	RINT	ANS
ES	ONI	AH
ZE	SH	HIANS

Samuel

Answers are in the back of the book.

WWJD?

Unscramble the place names in column A, then match the place with the relevant event in column B.

A	B
1. N A A C	a. Jesus' crucifixion
2. H E N B A T Y	b. Jesus healed Peter's mother-in-law
3. R A L C V A Y	c. Jesus entered riding a donkey
4. S H E G A M N E E T	d. Jesus raised Lazarus from the dead
5. L A U M R E E J S	e. Jesus' birthplace
6. A N C U P E R M A	f. Jesus' boyhood home
7. R A M A S I A	g. Jesus met a woman at the well
8. R E Z A T H A N	h. Jesus was betrayed with a kiss
9. M E T H E B L E H	i. Jesus changed water

Answers are in the back of the book.

Bible Crossword

Follow the clues!

			1	2	3			
			4					
			5					
6	7	8			9	10	11	12
13						14		
15			16		17			
			18	19				
			20					
			21					

Across

1. He left Sodom in a hurry
4. Did Noah need one?
5. MapQuest result (abbr.)
6. Shakespeare, for example
9. Jacob's brother
13. Commotion
14. Tavern beverage
15. Peter cast them
17. Jesus will do this
18. Jesus did this with His disciples before He died
20. Geese formation
21. Conger

Down

1. Jesus Christ
2. Horse morsel
3. One was in the middle of the Garden of Eden
6. Forbid
7. Summer beverage
8. Decay
10. Return mailer, acronym
11. Chicken ___ ___ king
12. Descendant of Bani (Ezra 10:34)
16. Jesus came to do this
17. Jacob grabbed this part of his brother's foot (Gen. 25:26)
19. Golf pin

Answers are in the back of the book.

Proverbial Endings

In the book of Proverbs, the author compares opposites. Pick the right word to complete the sentence! Chapter and verse appear in parentheses.

1. The fear of the LORD is the beginning of knowledge: but fools despise ___ (1:7)

   a. exercise b. health c. wisdom

2. Trust in the LORD with all thine heart; and lean not unto thine own ___ (3:5)

   a. understanding b. responsibilities c. day planner

3. He scorneth the scorners: but he giveth grace unto the ___ (3:34)

   a. lowly b. intelligent c. rich

4. Hatred stirreth up strifes: but love covereth all ___ (10:12)

   a. bodies b. worlds c. sins

5. A false balance is abomination to the LORD: but a just weight is his ___ (11:1)

   a. fear b. delight c. inspiration

6. The desire of the righteous is only good: but the expectation of the wicked is ___ (11:23)

   a. wealth b. wrath c. wrinkles

7. The fear of the Lord is the instruction of wisdom; and before honor is ___ (15:33)

   a. humility b. hilarity c. heaviness

Answers are in the back of the book.

Take a Trip to the Holy Land

You're planning a trip to the Holy Land, and there are many places you would like to visit. Match the location with the reason you would want to go there.

1. Nazareth	a. Place where Jesus prayed
2. Capernaum	b. Site of Joshua's victory
3. Bethlehem	c. Where Jesus calmed the storm
4. Jerusalem	d. Mary's well
5. Garden of Gethsemane	e. Lazarus' tomb
6. Bethany	f. Jesus' birthplace
7. Jericho	g. Where John baptized
8. Jordan River	h. Peter's mother-in-law's house
9. Sea of Galilee	i. Temple Mount

Answers are in the back of the book.

Biblical Sound Bites

Match the phrase with its speaker!

1. "Behold the man!"	a. Paul
2. "Wither thou goest, I will go."	b. Jesus
3. "I am the resurrection, and the life."	c. Ruth
4. "Let my people go."	d. Pilate
5. "Give me now wisdom and knowledge."	e. Moses
6. "Am I my brother's keeper?"	f. Satan
7. "Now abideth faith, hope, charity, these three; but the greatest of these is charity."	g. Soldier
8. "Yea, hath God said, Ye shall not eat of every tree of the garden?"	h. Angel
9. "Truly this man was the Son of God."	i. Cain
10. "He is risen, as he said."	j. Solomon

Answers are in the back of the book.

Cross-Offs

Cross off words according to directions given to reveal a communications tip.

Cross off:
1. fruits
2. conjunctions
3. months
4. animals
5. colors
6. deadly sins
7. fruits of the Spirit

KIND	BUT	PEACE
PEARS	PATIENCE	APRIL
MINK	CAT	GREED
MAY	WORDS	MOLE
BLUE	HUSKY	COME
APPLES	FAITH	FROM
JOY	CHERRIES	LOVING
AND	MARCH	SLOTH
ENVY	AZURE	FERRET
LOVE	HEARTS	PEACH

________ ________ ________ ________ ________ ________

Answers are in the back of the book.

Good Ideas

The Bible is full of people who revered the Lord and praised His name, even in spite of opposition. From the box below, find the godly person's name for each situation. Three names will not be used.

1. Remained true to God, despite woe and loss.
2. Continued to spread God's Word, despite shipwrecks, whippings, persecutions, and sickness.
3. Remained faithful to God throughout old age, despite the loss of a spouse after only seven years of marriage.
4. Believed God would provide an heir, despite being well past child-bearing years.
5. Believed God would forgive, despite having committed adultery and murder.
6. Continued to act out prophecies received from God, despite mockery and ridicule.
7. Sat at Jesus' feet, despite a sibling's ire.
8. Believed in Jesus, despite the disbelief of peers and colleagues.
9. Returned to his master, despite the possibility of severe punishment or death.

MARY	ONESIMUS	ANNA	DAVID
MARTHA	PAUL	ELIZABETH	EZEKIEL
NICODEMUS	PHILEMON	JOB	BOAZ

Answers are in the back of the book.

Bad Ideas

The Bible is full of people who chose to do wrong. From the box below, find the culprit's name for each situation. Three names will not be used.

1. Slew the prophets and was determined to murder Elijah.
2. Tried to hide from the Lord by boarding a ship bound for Tarshish.
3. Disobeyed God's command not to eat of a certain tree.
4. Denied even knowing Jesus when Jesus was on trial.
5. Organized a revolt against Moses.
6. Led a revolt against his father to take the throne.
7. Ordered the killing of infants in Bethlehem.
8. Betrayed Samson to his enemies.
9. Demanded the head of John the Baptist.

AHAZ	EVE	KORAH	BELSHAZZAR
JEZEBEL	DELILAH	JONAH	CAIN
PETER	HEROD	HERODIAS	ABSALOM

Answers are in the back of the book.

Word Search - Spiritual Riches

How rich are you–spiritually, that is? In this puzzle, see how many spiritual riches you can find. Words may read forward or backward; top to bottom or bottom to top; or diagonally. Cross off words in the word list as you find them.

Authenticity	Mercy
Contentment	Patience
Courtesy	Peace
Faith	Piety
Generosity	Prayer
Goodness	Purity
Grace	Respect
Gratitude	Strength
Hope	Tact
Joy	Trust
Justice	Virtue
Love	

C	G	O	L	P	U	R	I	T	Y	M	P	E
R	O	R	A	L	R	E	S	N	E	E	R	X
A	O	N	Y	O	J	C	O	N	A	R	O	E
Y	D	I	T	B	E	N	N	C	T	C	J	L
E	N	N	E	E	S	E	E	A	T	Y	E	O
S	E	F	I	L	N	I	T	N	O	A	S	V
H	S	R	P	A	O	T	O	G	R	A	C	E
O	S	A	S	I	C	A	M	R	A	M	I	T
P	R	U	V	N	O	P	A	E	Q	U	A	M
E	S	T	R	E	N	G	T	H	N	P	O	L
L	E	H	T	R	E	S	P	E	C	T	A	G
I	C	E	C	Y	N	O	A	L	R	S	A	E
K	I	N	D	N	E	S	S	O	T	U	N	N
A	T	T	I	O	L	R	E	Y	A	R	P	E
T	S	I	G	F	R	M	A	N	I	T	U	R
A	U	C	G	R	A	T	I	T	U	D	E	O
A	J	I	S	O	T	I	M	T	Q	O	M	S
E	U	T	R	I	V	N	T	A	P	P	R	I
B	E	Y	T	U	E	I	A	H	E	R	E	T
M	E	S	R	E	C	O	U	R	T	E	S	Y

Answers are in the back of the book.

Pass It On!

Many acts of tenderness and compassion are recorded in the Bible. Pick the correct person or place associated with each kindhearted act.

1. She adopted an infant she found in a basket left along the riverbank.
   a. Pharaoh's mother b. Pharaoh's aunt c. Pharaoh's daughter

2. She accompanied her mother-in-law to a foreign country rather than return to her family home.
   a. Orpah b. Ruth c. Naomi

3. He restored property to the disabled son of his beloved friend Jonathan.
   a. Saul b. Joshua c. David

4. Jesus restored the life of a widow's only son at the gates of this city.
   a. Nain b. Cana c. Jerusalem

5. She was one of many wealthy women who financially supported Jesus and His disciples.
   a. Lydia b. Dorcas c. Joanna

6. Jesus forgave Peter for denying Him during His hour of trial in this place
   a. High priest's palace b. Pilate's courtyard c. Mount Calvary

7. He provided a tomb for Jesus' body.
   a. Simon Peter b. Nicodemus c. Joseph of Arimathaea

Answers are in the back of the book.

NOT!

Cross out the one choice that does NOT belong!

1. Not a book of the Bible
   a. Jonah
   b. Job
   c. Josiah
   d. Jeremiah

2. Not one of Jesus' 12 disciples
   a. Peter
   b. Matthew
   c. Bartholomew
   d. Paul

3. Not a biblical miracle performed by Jesus
   a. Changing water into wine
   b. Walking on air
   c. Healing 10 lepers
   d. Raising Lazarus from the dead

4. Not one of the tribes of Israel
   a. Dan
   b. Asher
   c. Elijah
   d. Judah

5. Not an Old Testament prophet
   a. Paul
   b. Joel
   c. Amos
   d. Isaiah

6. Not a woman mentioned in the New Testament
   a. Dorcas
   b. Mary
   c. Joanna
   d. Ruth

Answers are in the back of the book.

Zig-Zags

A 7-letter word is hidden in each set of lines. The first letter of the answer may be the top or bottom letter of the first pair of letters; the second letter of the answer may be the top or bottom letter of the second pair of letters, and so on.

Example: BIBLES might look like this:

B	A	O	**L**	**E**	R
C	**I**	**B**	R	A	**S**

1.	P	H	I	M	O	S	E
	S	R	O	L	I	R	T
2.	S	I	G	A	L	S	H
	A	N	R	E	N	I	C
3.	F	O	I	E	N	E	S
	T	R	E	A	S	D	Y
4.	B	O	M	S	T	E	N
	P	L	E	R	S	A	D
5.	I	N	T	I	O	H	Y
	R	I	S	N	G	N	T

6.	P	L	R	G	E	N	E
	F	O	A	S	I	V	Y
7.	P	E	N	Y	S	R	E
	S	R	A	T	E	N	S
8.	H	I	R	V	A	N	Y
	T	E	A	N	E	T	S
9.	W	I	N	O	E	N	S
	S	A	T	N	R	S	T
10.	S	A	V	N	T	I	N
	H	E	I	R	A	L	Y
11.	A	S	C	S	S	A	L
	E	P	O	A	T	L	E
12.	D	O	N	K	S	E	Y
	C	A	U	N	A	R	L

Answers are in the back of the book.

Like What?

The Bible is full of word-pictures! Match each word-picture with its meaning.

1. Clanging cymbal	a. The tongue
2. Apples of gold in pictures of silver	b. Scripture
3. City on a hill	c. Faith
4. Rudder of a ship	d. Loveless person
5. Mustard seed	e. Well-spoken word
6. Wedding banquet	f. Godly People
7. Light for a path	g. Kingdom of heaven

Answers are in the back of the book.

Power of Elimination

Cross out words in the paragraph below to reveal a true saying.

RED YOU IDOLATRY CAN ACTS NAZARETH

GREEN PIN ACCOMPLISH PEAR PEW DECEIT

CANA MORE MATTHEW PULPIT IN GOLD

NEEDLE ONE BANANA HOUR JERUSALEM MURDER

WITH ORGAN TEAL GOD SPOOL PEACH

PURPLE JOEL THAN BETHANY IN ORANGE

THEFT ONE APPLE JUDE LIFETIME ALTAR

YELLOW THREAD WITHOUT ANTIOCH HIM

BLUE SCISSORS LUKE

CROSS OUT ALL:

1. FRUITS
2. BIBLE CITIES AND TOWNS
3. FURNISHINGS IN A CHURCH
4. SINS FORBIDDEN IN THE 10 COMMANDMENTS
5. COLORS
6. SEWING ACCESSORIES
7. NAMES OF BIBLE BOOKS

SAYING: ______________________________

Answers are in the back of the book.

In Other Words

For each fruit of the Holy Spirit, choose its opposite:

1. LOVE
a. wickedness b. hatred c. iniquity d. envy

2. JOY
a. sorrow b. spite c. impurity d. hatred

3. PEACE
a. hostility b. prosperity c. tumult d. gossip

4. PATIENCE
a. greed b. intolerance c. odium d. hostility

5. KINDNESS
a. annoyance b. hatred c. resentment d. cruelty

6. GOODNESS
a. anxiety b. resentment c. wickedness d. bitterness

7. FAITHFULNESS
a. infidelity b. malice c. anger d. cruelty

8. GENTLENESS
a. insensitivity b. roughness c. gluttony d. impurity

9. SELF-CONTROL
a. anger b. unkindness c. rudeness d. intemperance

Answers are in the back of the book.

It's a Zoo in Here!

All the critters got loose in Noah's ark! Help him sort out his menagerie by unscrambling the letters of each animal-word.

1. C L A M E

__ __ __ __ __

2. W A R P R O S

__ __ __ __ __ __ __

3. V O E D

__ __ __ __

4. P H E S E

__ __ __ __ __

5. C L I P A N E

__ __ __ __ __ __ __

6. P L E A T H E N

__ __ __ __ __ __ __ __

7. L U R E T T

__ __ __ __ __ __

8. O S O G E

__ __ __ __ __

Answers are in the back of the book.

Searching the Bible

Within the Bible-based sentences below, read the clues to find the hidden words. Words may appear anyplace in the sentence, reading left to right.

Example: The wall**s cam**e tumbling down.
Con game: scam

1. There was no room for them in the inn.
   Leaf for iced tea:__________
2. Jesus fed the crowd with five loaves and two fish.
   Seaside sight: __________
3. Moses never entered the Promised Land.
   High school event: __________
4. Agabus prophesied an event in Paul's life.
   A Scandinavian, perhaps: __________
5. On the third day, Jesus rose from the dead.
   WW II date: __________
6. The boy Jesus tarried in the temple.
   Celestial sight: __________
7. Of ten healed lepers, only one returned in gratitude to Jesus.
   Container: __________

Answers are in the back of the book.

Terrible Parables?

Each set of words is a rhyme or near rhyme of one of Jesus' parables. Can you guess which one? If you need a clue, check the Bible references!

The parable of the:

1. Frost Heap (Luke 15:3-7)

   ____

2. Keyed Lower (Mark 4:1-20)

   ____

3. Switch Spool (Luke 12:16-21)

   ____

4. Plate Beast (Luke 14:16-24)

   ____

5. Bossed Loin (Luke 15:8-10)

   ____

6. Creeds and Sleet (Matthew 13:24-30)

   ____

7. Sparrow War (Luke 13:22-30)

   ____

Answers are in the back of the book.

Mountain Climbing

By adding one letter and rearranging the letters to answer the clue, you can reach the top of the mountain!

SIR	Respectful title
STIR	Recipe instruction
TRIPS	Excursions
SPIRIT	SPIRIT

1

__ __	In the direction of
__ __ __	Cooking need
__ __ __ __	What you do at a red light
__ __ __ __ __	Schemes
__ __ __ __ __ __	Relating to mail service
APOSTLE	APOSTLE

2

__ __	Doubled, a way to say bye-bye
__ __ __	Dined
__ __ __ __	Story
__ __ __ __ __	Shoe grip
CATTLE	CATTLE

3

__ __

__ __ __

__ __ __ __

__ __ __ __ __

ANGELS

↑ Sixth tone of music scale

Beverage

Tilt

Gather bit by bit

ANGELS

4

__ __

__ __ __

__ __ __ __

__ __ __ __ __

CARMEL

↑ Summer cooler, for short

Pro

Spice related to nutmeg

Desert ride

CARMEL

5

__ __ __

__ __ __ __

__ __ __ __ __

__ __ __ __ __ __

SERPENT

↑ Look

Prophet

Scorn, with "at"

Primps

SERPENT

Answers are in the back of the book.

In a Word

In each Bible word, find the word that fits the clue.

Example: Barnabas – rural sight Answer: barn

1. Nehemiah – skirt feature ______
2. Creation – to dine ______
3. Announcements – building material ______
4. Covenant – diligent creature ______
5. Brokenhearted – museum display ______
6. Judas Iscariot – garage item ______
7. Compassionate – go ahead ______
8. Augustus Caesar – wind ______
9. Potiphar – clue ______
10. Philistine – series ______
11. Gomorrah – cheerleader's cry ______
12. Samaria – opera feature ______

Answers are in the back of the book.

Put-Togethers

In each word, find a word that matches the clue. Letters are in order, but separated.

Example: Jericho - Response from a shout, maybe

Answer: echo

1. Behemoth - two together ________________
2. Thessalonians - family guy ________________
3. Abraham - animal ________________
4. Atonement - camp closure ________________
5. Confession - penny ________________
6. Pomegranates - garden fixture ________________
7. Sycamore - long ago ________________
8. Priscilla - doctor's order ________________
9. Frankincense - Barbie's beau ________________

Answers are in the back of the book.

Books of the Bible Scramble

Unscramble the letters to reveal a book of the Bible; then unscramble the circled words to find another name for the Bible.

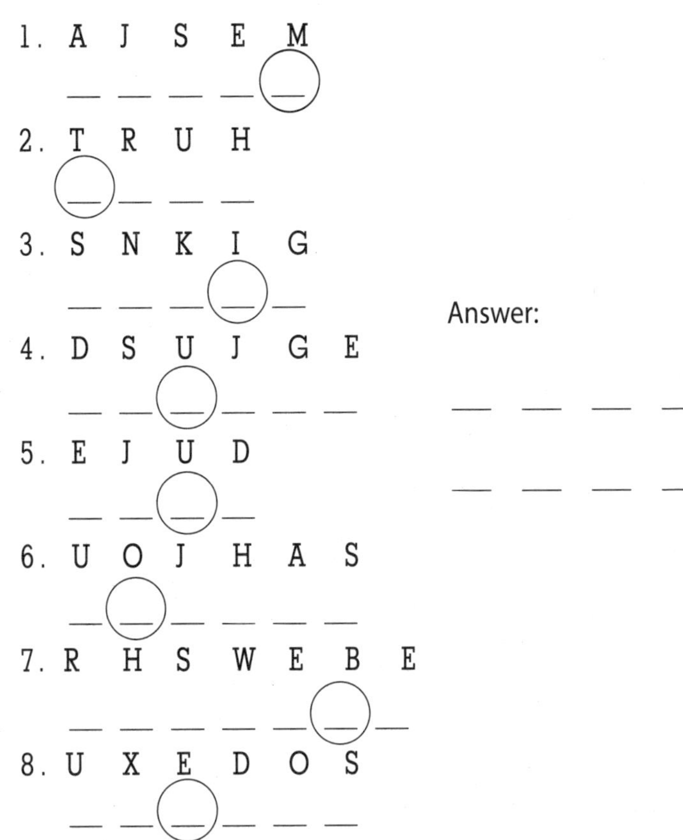

Hidden Tunes

Each silly sentence contains the title of an inspirational song. Can you find it?

1. Mama zinged by handily winning race.

 ____

2. I plead this, though: I came at once.

 ____

3. My crock pot offers room for two cabbages.

 ____

4. It's been shown that the greatest thousand people have heart.

 ____

5. I got Ellen a baseball mitt I won on their mountain bike.

 ____

6. Ah, is it thee? Ye missed at noon, yet another–gasp!–arrow.

 ____

7. Each morning, Abi, deliver wit, having a merry heart.

 ____

8. Ma, wayside inns, to a man, germs are inevitable.

 ____

Think It Through

The letters stacked in the top column go in the squares directly below the column, but not in the order given. Find where they fit to reveal an inspiring thought. Black squares indicate ends of words. The first word has been done for you.

P	O	N	E	S	S	E	L	W	I	S	R	S	H	E	K	T	O	I	T
T	H	E	D	T	H	O	O	H	S	H	E	T	E	E	E	H	H	R	I
Z	I	N		E	O		T	I	E	I			F	E	N	D		A	P
	U	N		F	R			V	E	R			F	I					
T	H	E	■								■					■			
						■					■				■				
			■				■					■					■		
■						■						■					■	■	■

Round We Go!

Start at the heart and work clockwise to find all the words you can without skipping letters. We found 17 words.

Say What?

Many words and expressions have their source in the Bible. Pick the correct meaning of each word or phrase.

1. JEREMIAD
a. opinion b. harangue c. debate

2. SIMONY
a. buying or selling a church rank or position
b. beating or whipping a person
c. believing in or practicing sorcery

3. A JUDAS
a. a thief b. a liar c. a betrayer

4. TO WASH ONE'S HANDS OF
a. to disassociate oneself from
b. to remove germs from c. to wipe dirt from

5. CARRY A CROSS
a. lug something heavy b. bear a mark c. endure a hardship

6. SCAPEGOAT
a. sickly farm animal b. blame-bearer c. stubborn person

7. SALT OF THE EARTH
a. faithful people b. risqué people c. seafaring people

Answers are in the back of the book.

Pick a Letter

In each of the letter-pairs below, find a five-letter word by picking a letter from the top or bottom row.

Example:

M	**I**	**G**	R	**T**
L	O	A	**H**	B

Light

1.

F	S	I	N	G
S	A	C	T	H

2.

L	O	B	I	E
B	I	M	L	S

3.

S	O	A	W	N
L	E	S	R	E

4.

C	R	E	T	D
B	O	M	A	N

5.

P	L	O	C	K
S	E	A	T	E

6.

P	O	L	M	R
V	I	W	E	S

7.

G	M	O	R	E
E	L	A	T	Y

1. __________
2. __________
3. __________
4. __________
5. __________
6. __________
7. __________

Answers are in the back of the book.

ANSWERS

PAGE 6/7

```
H E A R D M O R E D O N
Q U N A E B I R K S N I
N L A Z A R U S N A O M
N E A R F A N E C C L E
S H E P H I C A L M E D
N O L B O S Y E W C R O
T H E A L E D M A J O B
A N P L C D E A L O N A
E Y E S R A S E K W O W
T H R A O L A M E A B A
C O S W W E H U D Y E T
O N F E D A N T W I N E
T H E S P O K E C O O R
```

PAGE 8

1. F 2. T (Isaiah 40:15) 3. F 4. T (Proverbs 16:18) 5. F 6. F 7. F 8. T (Job 19:20) 9. F 10. F 11. F 12. T (Ecclesiastes 10:20)

PAGE 9

PAGE 10

1. Kings
2. Disciples
3. Prophets
4. Noah's sons
5. Siblings
6. Priests
7. Family Members
8. Fishermen
9. Missionaries

PAGE 11

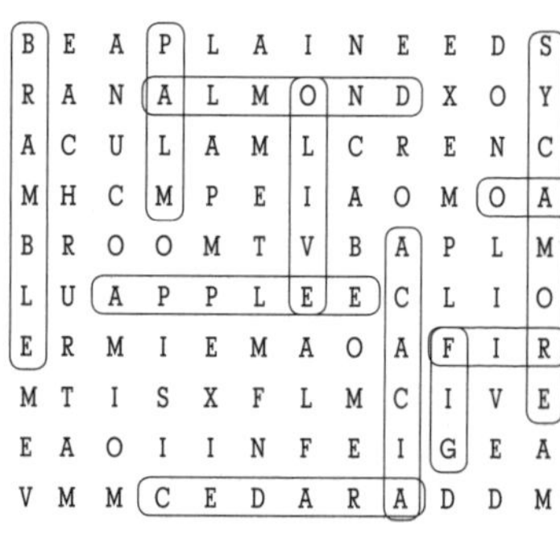

PAGE 12

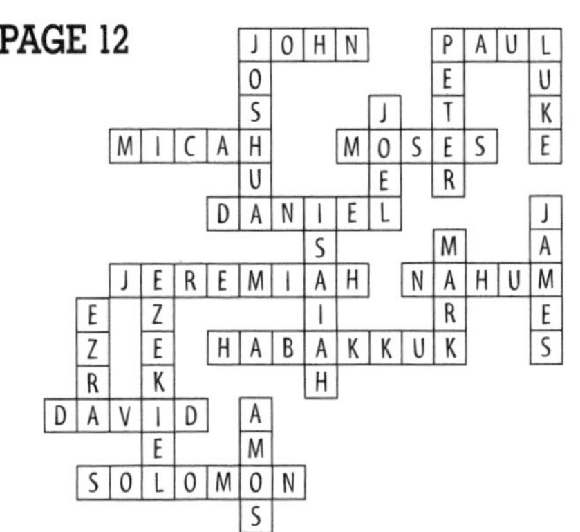

PAGE 13

1. (c) Korah (Numbers 16:1) 2. (a) Saul (1 Samuel 19:10) 3. (b) Ahaz (2 Chronicles 28:1-3) 4.(d) Haman (Esther 3-7) 5. (b) Herod (Matthew 14:1-11) 6. (b) Judas Iscariot (John 6:70-71)

PAGE 14/15

1) Arm is moved in second pew. 2) Lady's earring is missing. 3) Man has glasses on. 4) Pastor's arm is moved. 5) Right flower pot has an extra flower.

PAGE 16/17

PAGE 18

1. b 2. c 3. b 4. a
5. a 6. c 7. c 8. a
9. c 10. a 11. b 12. a

ANSWERS

PAGE 19

```
T R O P L M N U Y H T A R F E D
S T F B R D E W S X A L A A B N
T U T J P T B O P L M M U Y N Y
U B N F M E L M E P I S T L E P
D U E I A N N T B R C E W E Q S
Y L M B N C E T G S D I Y T T M
O Y U V N W Q F A M E N Y T V O
F G R W A B U B E T B T R E Y N
E O T W S X B O I R E E M R M E
N L S C D A W M I Y T U T B O Y
D O N I T Y T B R I V A C P D T
T T I H J L P O M N I O S H G O
I A L L E R B M I T F E O R N T
M H A D U J N O L I M P G O I H
E C C H B T C V E O D B O N K E
S S I N H U J P A R A B L E D P
B E S C F D A Y O F R E S T N O
H B U T G O T W R E D K I M A O
L K M H G F O S S Q W E O T L R
E C R D T Y H D I T M O L L Y K
F I R S T F I V E B O O K S L D
V R F B G T M U J Y N R G B O K
O L P K I I D O L B U B Y Y H R
```

PAGE 20

```
Y G T S I T P A B E H T N H O J
R V E D U N T C R V R D E H M I
N T F E L T G H J L I O A U I O
U Y J N U E X W D Y N O L M I J
N J O N A H D C U K N H S G Y N
H F B S P X Z P O M L K I H U N
Y B T V C E S W O A L O M I U H
H B Y T S A M S O N L C I M O A
L J J H G F E S A E W E R T V J
E C E D T S H N U J M O L M I I
P L O S G T Y M E C W S X C E L
V L F B U M A H A R B A G R I E
O U P K I S Y N G B U B E Y V R
D A V I D A D F A K E T F M I P
F S N U G T D A N I E L I M O L
Y R V E O U Y N T P A F M N V C
D V W O M I K L P L T G V N B H
```

PAGE 21 (Answers will var

PAGE 22

1. God places... 2. Noah builds... 3. Abraham... 4. Joseph .... 5. Ten Commandments... 6. King David... 7. Solomon's... 8. Gabriel... 9. John the Baptist... 10. Jesus is baptized... 11. Jesus teaches... 12. Jesus dies... 13. Paul spreads... 14. The Apostle John...

PAGE 23

simon, james or phillip, matthew, peter, andrew, john

PAGE 24

In all thy ways acknowledge him, and he shall direct thy paths. Proverbs 3:6 KJV

PAGE 25

1 - D, 2 - G, 3 - A, 4 - F, 5 - B, 6 - C, 7 - E —1 - C, 2 - G, 3 - A, 4 - F, 5 - D, 6 - B, 7 - E

PAGE 26/27

1. b, 2. a, 3. b, 4. b, 5. c, 6. a, 7. c, 8. b, 9. a, 10. b, 11. c, 12. b

PAGE 28

Lo, I am with you always. Matthew 28:20 KJV

PAGE 29

- Messiah, 2 - Nazarene, 3 - Redeemer, 4 - Mediator,
- Counselor, 6 - Alpha, 7 - Emmanuel

PAGE 30

. a (Genesis 3:15) 2. c (Luke 2:36-38) 3. c (Acts 9:40)
. b (Genesis 30:21) 5. b (Ruth 1:15-17) 6. a (2 Kings 22:14)
c (Mark 16:9)

PAGE 31

- b (Genesis 26:5),
- a (1 Samuel 7:12).
- c (John 1:41),
- a (John 9:7),
- c (Exodus 20:10-11),
- b (John 14:26),
- c (Titus 3:7),
- b (Colossians 4:16)

PAGE 32/33

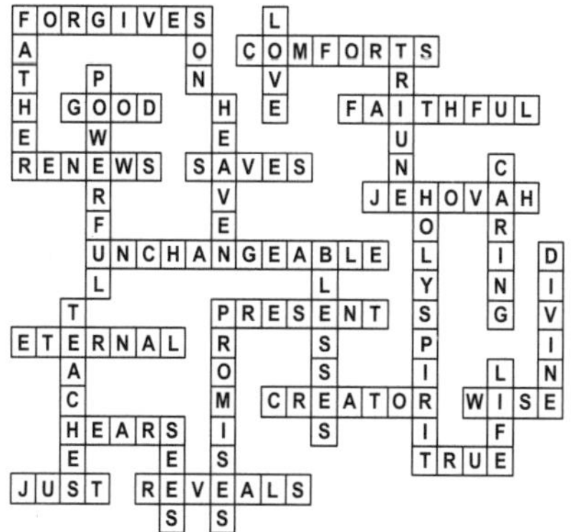

ANSWERS

PAGE 34/35

1) Lady in the background is moved. 2) Little boy is looking the other way. 3) Sign is lower. 4) Woman in the middle is wearing an earring. 5) Lady's dress is longer.

PAGE 36

1. ARK (GENESIS 7:1) 2. COLT (MARK 11:7)
3. CHARIOT (ACTS 8:28-31) 4. BOAT (MATTHEW 14:29)
5. FISH (JONAH 1:17) 6. LADDER (GENESIS 28:12)
7. CAMEL (GENESIS 24:61) 8. HORSE (REVELATION 6:2)

PAGE 37

B. Abel, Noah, Jacob, Matthew, Paul C. Lot, Amos, King Herod Jesus, Timothy D. Joshua, David, Solomon, Micah, Luke

PAGE 38

PAGE 39

1. a 2. a 3. b 4. c
5. b 6. b 7. c

PAGE 40

(Answers will vary)

I
A**S**P
ST**R**UM
MAC**A**DAM
STON**E**WALL
UNWIL**L**INGL

ANSWERS

PAGE 41

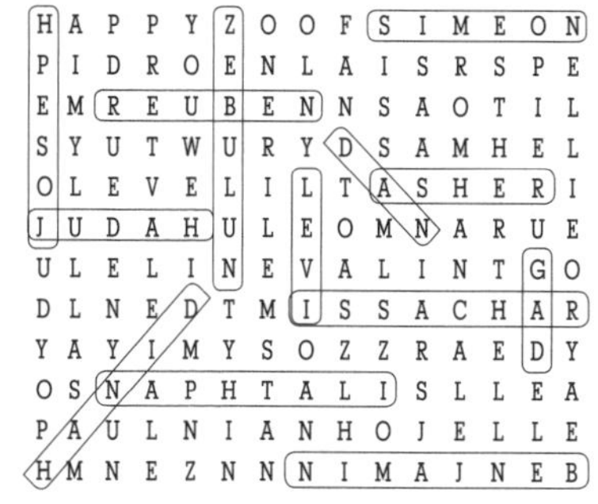

PAGE 42/43

PAGE 46/47

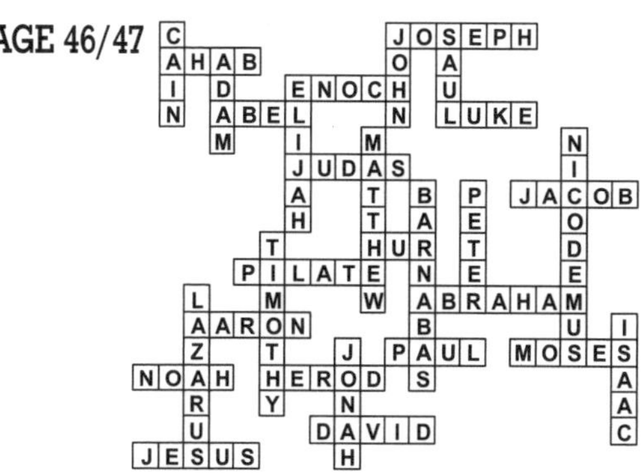

PAGE 44

1. JERICHO
2. BABEL
3. NAZARETH
4. TARSUS
5. PERGA
6. MOAB
7. EMMAUS
8. JERUSALEM
9. NINEVEH
10. ENOCH

PAGE 45

1. b (Matthew 13:31)
2. d (Ruth 2:23)
3. a (John 1:48)
4. d (Matthew 3:4)
5. a (Luke 22:17, 19)
6. b (Matthew 14:17)

PAGE 48

Judges, Ruth, Acts, Numbers, Mark, Lamentations, James, Revelation, Job, Kings, Psalms, Proverbs, Luke, Esther

PAGE 49

1) Cornelius (Acts 10:1) 2) Zephaniah (Zephaniah 1:1) 3) Alexander (2 Timothy 4:14) 4) Methuselah (Genesis 5:25) 5) Bathsheba (2 Samuel 11:3) 6) Bartimaeus (Mark 10:46) 7) Ahasuerus (Esther 1:1) 8) Elimelech (Ruth 1:2)

PAGE 50

I can do all things through Christ which strengtheneth me. Philippians 4:13 KJV

PAGE 51

God is love. 1 John 4:16 KJV

PAGE 52/53

1) Arches are lower. 2) Pastor's nose is smaller. 3) Book is larger. 4) Bride's dress is smaller. 5) Woman in the front pew has hand moved.

PAGE 54/55

PAGE 56

1 - e (John 6:5-13),
2 - g (1 Kings 3:16-28),
3 - a (Mark 5:35-42),
4 - f (Acts 12:13),
5 - b (Exodus 2:10),
6 - i (Luke 2:46-47),
7 - c (John 4:46-53),
8 - d (1 Samuel 1:24-28),
9 - h (Genesis 21:3)

PAGE 57

```
O L H A N N A H G B U B H Y V R
P E W S X A D F H N A O M I F A
F R U T H T W N U U Y B I M O L
E V E A A U Y N L X R A C H E L
D V N O P I K L D T T G V N L I
Y I T M R D E S A A Q A E E I C
D V E A O N T B H T R L E S Z S
N T F R Y T I H J L A O M T A I
U Y C T V T X A D D N M M H B R
N A V H H E H R G E O H A E E P
S N E A Q T Z A G B L K I R T N
Y N T V I E M S Q O L O R I H U
H A Y T G Y T H R R M C I M O M
L O J H R F A N N A W E M T V A
E J R A T E H N I H M O R M I R
P L M B L T R E B E K A H C E Y
V R J U D I T H J Y N T G B I K
```

PAGE 58

1. c. Naomi (in-law) 2. a. Mary (sister) 3. b. Onesimus (master) 4. d. Abraham (grandson) 5. b. Miriam (brother) 6. c. Michal (husband) 7. a. Isaac (wife)

PAGE 59

Deborah	d. Judge (Judges 4:4)
Paul	f. Tentmaker (Acts 18:3)
Baruch	h. Scribe (Jeremiah 36:4)
Luke	i. Physician (Colossians 4:14)
Zacchaeus	b. Tax Collector (Luke 19:2)
Lydia	g. Merchant (Acts 16:14)
Andrew	c. Fisher (Matthew 4:18)
Amos	a. Shepherd (Amos 1:1)
Dorcas	e. Tailor (Acts 9:39)

PAGE 60

Samuel

PAGE 61 (Answers will vary)

1. tent 2. Abba 3. dead 4. Miriam 5. Nain
6. David 7. Eagle 8. acacia 9. widow
10. ruler 11. deed 12. river

PAGE 62/63

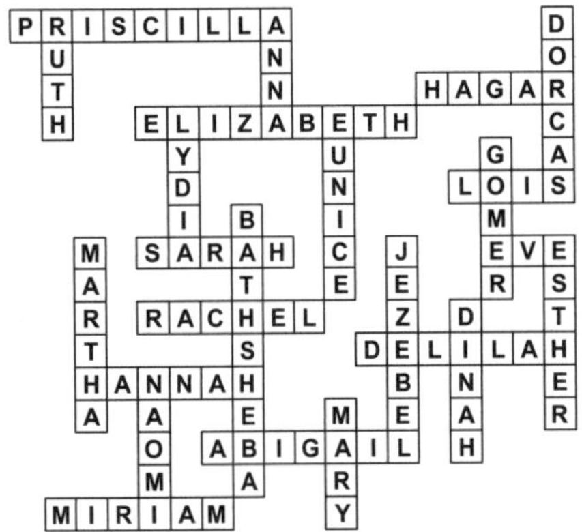

PAGE 64/65

1) Lampshade is larger. 2) Arm on chair is different. 3) Young Girl's eyebrows are missing. 4) Young Girls pants are longer. 5) Table has moved closer.

PAGE 66

1. (a) 2. (c) 3. (a) 4. (b) 5. (c) 6. (a)

PAGE 67

Andrew

PAGE 68/69

1) Church has one less window. 2) Stop sign is shorter. 3) Car grill is different. 4) Girl's pony tail is gone. 5) Mirror is gone.

PAGE 70

Ask and ye shall receive that your joy may be full.
John 16:24 KJV

PAGE 71

1. b. (Genesis 19:17, 26) 2. a., c. (Genesis 39:7-20)
3. d. (Judges 16:4-20) 4. b., c. (1 Kings 18:19, 18:13)
5. a., c., d. (Matthew 14:3-11)

PAGE 72

Speak for thy servant heareth. 1 Samuel 3:10 KJV

PAGE 73

bushel, barley, cubits, Red Sea, donkey, church, Sunday

PAGE 74/75

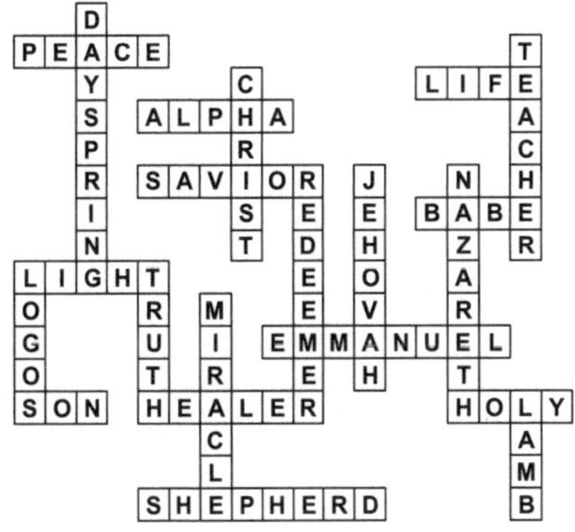

PAGE 76

Haggai, Philemon, Galatians, Obadiah, Ecclesiastes, Hebrews, Philippians, Habakkuk, Nahum, Psalms, Timothy, Colossians

PAGE 77

O O W L S O M E U M E L O O K S A W
I S E E K S A A R O N E N S U I G E
B R E E A S T C A O R N B E A D R S
C E P J T O T C L H A G G A I I E S
A A S P E N H E E D B E O O D E E D
V R A Y M T E Q U E S M P O R T D O
R A C L A I W R E S S O M M D R I M
E C C L E S I A S T E S E E T T L E
J E U V E A X T C O L O S S I A N S
S U S S E A I A R R N O T R P R I H
E T E R C C O H A B A K K U K E O E
S T R O O P B E E R S H E B A A N E
R E S U F F E R I C C A E P R M I P
P L U G G E P H I L I P P I A N S O
A I L A A G E W C O Z Z I L L E E D
F U L F I L L M E N T E P L L E E V
I U A F H E L E W E O D P A O T L O

PAGE 78/79

1) Bricks by window are missing.
2) Lady's leg has moved. 3) Hat has a band on it.
4) Steps have moved
5) Tree has moved.

PAGE 80/81

Let these gifts to us be blessed. Amen

PAGE 82/83

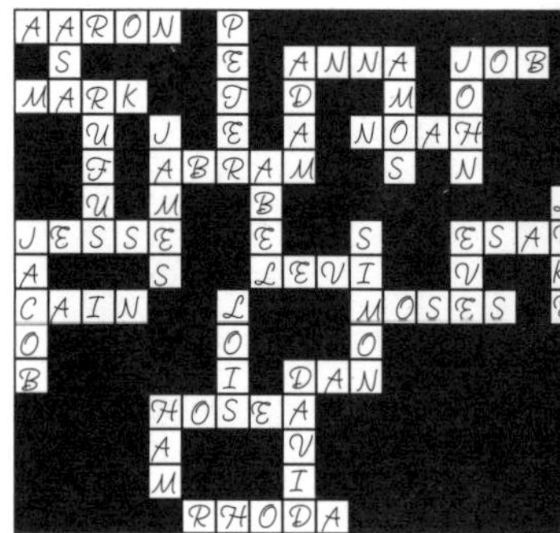

PAGE 84/85

1) Robe is shorter. 2) Manger has moved down. 3) Brick on the right is missing. 4) Windows on dome are different. 5) Star is smaller.

PAGE 86

```
L W E D D I N G F E A S T M I T
N W E W S E D C U K O H H G E N
H I E S Q X E P O M L K E K U N
Y S D E E W E H T A L O S I N S
H E Y T G V R F R E D A O M O U
L M J H G F T S A Q B E W T V R
E A U D T Y G N I A M O E M I A
P N O S G T I F R C W S R C E Z
V S F B T T F E J Y N T G B I A
O F P K I A D P E E H S T S O L
P O W S X N R F A K D P F M N D
F U N U U T W D O U Y B I M O N
Y N V P O U Y N S X A F M N S A
D D M O M I K L P E T G V N L N
Y A T F R D E S W A E A M H A A
L T E D U N T C R V R D E I G M
N I E R U S A E R T N E D D I H
G O O D S A M A R I T A N B D C
O N P K I M Y N G B U B H Y O I
W E W S X A D F A K D P F M R R
F E N U G T W N O U Y B I M P L
```

PAGE 87

The eyes of the LORD are upon the righteous, and his ears are open unto their cry.
Psalm 34:15 KJV

PAGE 88

```
N T F B Y T G H J T A N G U I O
A D D E R E X W D Y N O L M D J
N Y V A S A D L M K E H B G R N
H F D R I B O P O L L A I J A N
Y B T V F C X B T A L O G I P U
H B Y L U G N E T H S I F L O P
L S O S G F E S A E W E O T E R
E W T N T B S P A R R O W N L T
F A N U E T E N O O Y B I M O U
F L V E O V L H E N A F M N V R
D L B O M I A L E L T L T N B T
Y O E L R D H R A M Q A M H I L
R W E A U N W C R V O C T M E E
P L O M G T Y F E G W T X C E D
V R F B G T M U V Y L T H B I O
O L P K Y E K N O D U B P S A V
P C A M E L D F D K D P F M I E
```

PAGE 89

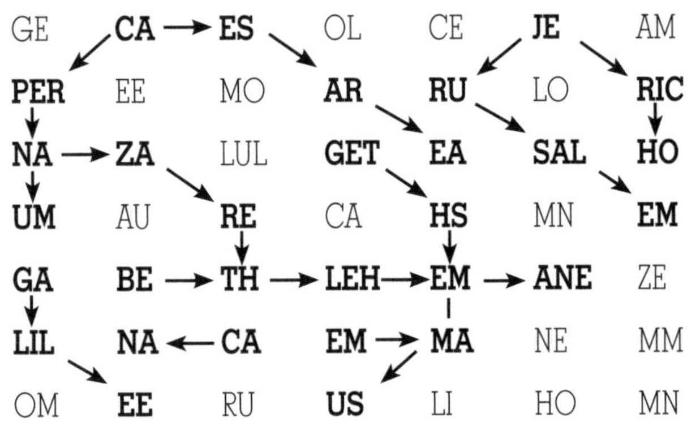

PAGE 90/91

BIBLE PLACES: 1 - B, 2 - G, 3 - A, 4 - H, 5 - I, 6 - D, 7 - E, 8 - F, 9 -
BIBBLE PEOPLE: 1-G, 2 - E, 3 - I, 4 - H, 5 - A, 6 - D, 7 - C, 8 - B, 9 -

PAGE 92/93

1) Boy in front row has a different tie. 2) Boy in back row eyes closed. 3) Girl's hand in back row has moved. 4) Choir teacher arm has moved. 5) Bands on sleeve are missing.

PAGE 94

1. star / rats, 2. dew / wed, 3. keep / peek, 4. ten / net, 5. bard / drab, 6. rood / door, 7. step / pets, 8. war / raw, 9. nib / bin, 10. loop / pool, 11. sleep / peels, 12. pal / lap, 13. mad / dam, 14. tops / spot

PAGE 95 (Answers will vary. Here's our list:)

true, sate, gate, soak, soon, moon, tame, neat, rage, meat, soar, rare, tare, gear, sane, sage, none, tram

PAGE 96/97

1. HEAVENS, MOON, STARS
2. EARTH
3. TREE, RIVERS
4. MOON, SUN
5. HEAVEN, EARTH, SEAS
6. EARTH, MOUNTAINS, SEA
7. EARTH, HILLS
8. CLOUDS, SKIES
9. FIELD, TREES, WOOD

PAGE 98

1. Fine
2. Rest
3. Address
4. Nice
5. Cast
6. Issue
7. Sewer

Saint's Name:
Francis

PAGE 99

O L P K I E Y N G B U B H Y V R

P J W S X A M F A K D P F M I P

F E N U G T W M O T A R S U S L

Y R C A P E R N A U M F M N N C

D U W N M I K L P U A G V N A A

Y S T T R D E P H A S U S H Z P

R A E I U N T C R V C D E S A P

N L F O B T G H J L U O M U R O

U E H C V E X H D E S O L M E J

N M V H S E T C U K R H B G T N

H F E S Q N Z H O M L I I J H N

Y B T V I E S W L A L O C I N U

H B Y R G V A F T E D C I H O P

L K O H G F N S Y Q H E R T O R

E C R D T Y A E R A S E A C I K

P L O B G T C F E C W S M C E D

V R F B G T M U J Y N T G B I K

PAGE 100/101

1. b, 2. a,
3. c, 4. b,
5. c, 6. a,
7. c, 8. c,
9. a, 10. b,
11. b, 12. c,
13. a, 14. b

PAGE 102/103

1. 1 Corinthians 13–the great "love chapter" of Paul's letter to the Corinthians.
2. Cain's response to God when God inquired about his murdered brother.
3. The first words of Psalm 23, the "Shepherd Psalm."
4. Pontius Pilate's words to the crowd as he presented to them Jesus, bleeding.
5. Moses' words to Pharaoh, pleading for the release of the Israelites.
6. The angel Gabriel's words to Mary announcing her role in the birth of Jesus.
7. Ruth's words to her mother-in-law after both women were widowed.
8. Jesus' question to Judas Iscariot.
9. Mordecai's question to Queen Esther as he pleads for her help.
10. Adam's words to Eve in the Garden of Eden.
11. Joseph's words to Potiphar's wife.
12. Jesus' commandment to Peter after Jesus' resurrection.

PAGE 104

Let us hold fast the profession of our faith without wavering; for he is faithful that promised.
Hebrews 10:23 KJV

PAGE 105

1. The Israelites celebrate... 2. After 430 years in Egypt
3. The Israelites cross the Red Sea... 4. God sends manna
5. Moses receives the Ten Commandments from God
6. Aaron makes a golden calf... 7. Out of anger,
8. Moses receives the Commandments a second time (Exodus 34:28) 9. The Israelites build... 10. Moses dies 11. Joshua sends spies... 12. Joshua leads the Israelites

PAGE 106

```
T O S N A P D R A G O N I N G
B E A M S Z D A F F O D I L I
U M Z S E N E S L I L U R S N
T E A U T I V A I N E D R A G
T N L M O E O I V I O L E T S
A R E C Q U R L P O R D S I S
O C A R N A T I O N H A I A W
N P W I T I N G S I R I S E E
P E T L L I L Y E M I S P I E
A T U M I N S P A N S Y E U T
Z U L I A L U M S O E S O N P
I N I A S O A L I R I N N S E
R I P E N S Y C P O P P Y P A
M A R I G O L D C S I C O R I
U C Z I N N I A M E N O S I S
M A M S S T E N N O B E U L B
```

PAGE 107

1 - e,
2 - g,
3 - a,
4 - i,
5 - j,
6 - b,
7 - h,
8 - c,
9 - f,
10 - d

PAGE 108

1. Continue in... Colossians 4:2 2. Trust...Proverbs 3:5
3. Come...Matthew 11:28 4. A wise...Proverbs 1:5
5. Wait...Psalm 27:14 6. I am...John 6:35
7. The Lord...Numbers 6:24

PAGE 109

1 - Nathanael, Peter, Andrew; 2 - Melchizedek, Eli, Samuel; 3 - Judah, Gilgal, Galilee; 4 - Genesis, Judges, Psalms; 5 - Corinthians, Romans, Galatians; 6 - Ruth, Esther, Rebekah; 7 - John, Matthew, Luke; 8 - Elizabeth, Mary, Leah; 9 - Ahab, David, Herod; 10 - Elijah, Amos, Ezekiel; 11 - Naomi, Orpah, Anna; 12 - Paul, Daniel, Joseph

PAGE 110/111

Parable: Prodigal Son, Loyal Father

G	N	I	R	R	T	W	O
P	S	E	R	V	A	N	T
S	R	S	F	S	I	N	S
A	I	O	S	E	A	M	Y
Y	L	N	D	G	A	V	E
F	L	A	C	I	I	S	S
A	L	I	V	E	G	P	T
F	L	S	K	I	D	A	Y
O	O	I	I	S	A	D	L
U	Y	R	S	O	R	R	Y
N	A	E	S	R	O	B	E
D	L	F	A	T	H	E	R

PAGE 112/113

PAGE 114

Answers: (Yours may vary.) cask, clad, clam, cram, dais, dame, dead, dear, dock, lack, lame, mare, mask, orca, rack , road, roam, roar, rock, rode, same, sire

PAGE 115

1 - b, 2 - a, 3 - d, 4 - c, 5 - a, 6 - c, 7 - b, 8 - a

PAGE 116

1. b 2. a 3. b 4. a 5. c 6. c 7. b 8. a 9. b 10. c

PAGE 117

1. b (Genesis 30:20-21), 2. a (2 Samuel 12:24),
3. c (Numbers 26:59), 4. b (Matthew 1:5), 5. a (Genesis 4:25),
6. b (1 Samuel 1:20), 7. b (2 Timothy 1:5), 8. c (Mark 16:1),
9. a (Matthew 1:16)

PAGE 118

1. c (Genesis 4:9), 2. a (Matthew 19:18-19), 3. b (John 19:5),
4. a (Luke 1:38) 5. c (Matthew 5:1-9), 6. b (Acts 3:6),
7. c (Esther 4:15-16)

PAGE 119

A soft answer turns away wrath. Proverbs 15:1

PAGE 120/121

A - Peter (Mark 14:72),
B - Sarah (Genesis 17:17; 18:10), C - Simeon and Anna (Luke 2:25-38), D - David (1 Samuel 17:49), E - Paul (Acts 9:1-6), F - Noah (Genesis 7:1), G - Ruth (Ruth 4:13), H - Martha (Luke 10:41-42)

PAGE 122/123

			1 E	2 L	3 I			
			4 D	O	C			
			5 E	L	K			
6 L	7 O	8 I	N	■	9 Y	10 A	11 R	12 N
13 I	N	N	■	■	■	14 S	U	E
15 B	O	A	16 Z	■	17 R	A	N	T
			18 E	19 V	E			
			20 R	O	E			
			21 O	W	L			

PAGE 124

E	N	O	K	R	A	M	O	S	O	L	I
I	Z	A	H	O	S	A	R	O	J	V	A
T	O	R	D	M	A	L	E	J	O	E	L
I	O	N	A	A	V	A	H	E	B	U	P
T	I	A	N	N	J	C	T	R	K	J	E
U	T	H	I	S	O	H	S	E	C	U	T
S	H	U	E	U	N	I	E	M	L	D	E
G	O	M	L	B	A	K	N	I	H	E	R
N	S	N	A	E	H	P	S	A	L	M	S
I	E	O	G	A	I	E	U	H	K	A	M
K	A	C	T	S	W	O	W	J	O	H	N
S	A	V	I	O	R	A	H	S	A	L	M

PAGE 125

1 - b,
2 - a,
3 - c,
4 - c,
5 - b,
6 - a

PAGE 126/127

1 - c, 2 - a, 3 - c, 4 - b, 5 - d, 6 - d, 7 - b, 8 - a, 9 - c, 10 - b

PAGE 128

1. The Flood - c. Noah, 2. Pentecost - g. Peter, 3. The Fall - e. Adam and Eve, 4. Sermon on the Mount - a. Jesus, 5. Destruction of Sodom - f. Lot, 6. Exodus from Egypt - b. Moses, 7. Battle of Jericho - d. Joshua

PAGE 129

1. Samson, 2. Paul, 3. Baruch, 4. Covenant, 5. Israel, 6. Adar 7. Joseph, 8. Hezekiah, 9. Andrew

PAGE 130

1. c,b 2. c,a 3. b,c 4. b,a 5. a,c

PAGE 131

1. a 2. b 3. a 4. c 5. a 6. b 7. c

PAGE 132

1. b 2. c 3. a 4. b 5. c 6. b 7. c

PAGE 133

Possible Answers: hen, hay, eel, van, yen, eye, aye, yea, any, nave, have, lave, vane, even, heave, leave, leaven, heavy, heal, heel, veal

PAGE 134

Samuel, Corinthians, Timothy, Obadiah, Chronicles, Joshua, Proverbs, Philemon, Haggai, Galatians, Hebrews, Esther, Zechariah

PAGE 135

1. Cana, i
2. Bethany, d
3. Calvary, a
4. Gethsemane, h
5. Jerusalem, c
6. Capernaum, b
7. Samaria, g
8. Nazareth, f
9. Bethlehem, e

PAGE 136/137

			1 L	2 O	3 T			
			4 O	A	R			
			5 R	T	E			
6 B	7 A	8 R	D	■	9 E	10 S	11 A	12 U
13 A	D	O	■	■	■	14 A	L	E
15 N	E	T	16 S	■	17 H	E	A	L
			18 A	19 T	E			
			20 V	E	E			
			21 E	E	L			

PAGE 138

1. c 2. a 3. a 4. c 5. b 6. b 7. a

PAGE 139

1. Nazareth - d. Mary's well, 2. Capernaum - h. Peter's mother-in-law's house, 3. Bethlehem - f. Jesus' birthplace, 4. Jerusalem - i. Temple Mount, 5. Garden of Gethsemane - a. Place where Jesus prayed, 6. Bethany - e. Lazarus' tomb, 7. Jericho - b. Site of Joshua's victory, 8. Jordan River - g. Where John baptized, 9. Sea of Galilee - c. Where Jesus calmed the storm

PAGE 140

1. d. (John 19:5), 2. c. (Ruth 1:16), 3. b. (John 11:25),
4. e. (Exodus 5:1), 5. j. (2 Chronicles 1:10), 6. i. (Genesis 4:9),
7. a. (1 Corinthians 13:13), 8. f. (Genesis 3:1), 9. g. (Mark 15:39)
10. h. (Matthew 28:6)

PAGE 141

Kind words come from loving hearts.

PAGE 142

1. Job 2. Paul 3. Anna 4. Elizabeth 5. David
6. Ezekiel 7. Mary 8. Nicodemus 9. Onesimus

PAGE 143

1. Jezebel 2. Jonah 3. Eve 4. Peter 5. Korah
6. Absalom 7. Herod 8. Delilah 9. Herodias

PAGE 144/145

PAGE 146

1. c. 2. b.
3. c. 4. c.
5. b. 6. b.
7. c.

PAGE 147

1. c. 2. d.
3. b. 4. c.
5. a. 6. d.

PAGE 148/149

1. Promise, 2. Angelic, 3. Friends, 4. Blessed
5. Insight, 6. Forgive, 7. Prayers, 8. Heavens,
9. Witness 10. Saintly, 11. Apostle, 12. Counsel

PAGE 150

1. Clanging cymbal, d. 2. Apples of gold in pictures of silver, e.
3. City on a hill, f. 4. Rudder of a ship, a. 5. Mustard seed, c.
6. Wedding banquet, g. 7. Light for a path, b.

PAGE 151

You can accomplish more in one hour with God than in one lifetime without Him.

PAGE 152

1 - b, 2 - a, 3 - c, 4 - b, 5 - d, 6 - c, 7 - a, 8 - b, 9 - d

PAGE 153

1. Camel, 2. Sparrow, 3. Dove, 4. Sheep, 5. Pelican, 6. Elephant, 7. Turtle, 8. Goose

PAGE 154

1. There was no room for the**m in t**he inn.
2. Jesus fed the crowd with five loave**s and** two fish.
3. Moses never entered the **Prom**ised Land.
4. Agabus prophesie**d an e**vent in Paul's life.
5. On the thir**d day**, Jesus rose from the dead.
6. The boy Jesu**s tar**ried in the temple.
7. Of ten healed lepers, only one ret**urn**ed in gratitude to Jesus.

PAGE 155

1. Lost Sheep 2. Seed Sower 3. Rich Fool 4. Great Feast
5. Lost Coin 6. Weeds and Wheat 7. Narrow Door

PAGE 156/157

1.
TO
POT
STOP
PLOTS
POSTAL
APOSTLE

2.
TA
ATE
TALE
CLEAT
CATTLE

3.
LA
ALE
LEAN
GLEAN
ANGELS

4.
AC
ACE
MACE
CAMEL
CARMEL

5.
SEE
SEER
SNEER
PREENS
SERPENT

PAGE 158

1. hem, 2. eat, 3. cement, 4. ant, 5. art, 6. car, 7. pass, 8. gust, 9. tip, 10. list, 11. rah, 12. aria

PAGE 159

1. both, 2. son, 3. ram, 4. tent, 5. coin, 6. gate, 7. yore, 8. pill, 9. Ken

PAGE 160

JAMES, RUTH, KINGS, JUDGES, JUDE, JOSHUA, HEBREWS, EXODUS
Book Name: GOD'S WORD

PAGE 161

1. Amazing Grace, 2. Lead Thou Me On, 3. Rock of Ages,
4. How Great Thou Art, 5. Go Tell It on the Mountain,
6. His Eye Is on the Sparrow, 7. Abide with Me,
8. Away in a Manger

PAGE 162

The foolish seek happiness over the horizon; the wise find it under their feet.

PAGE 163

care, car, are, return, turn, urn, not, other, the, her, others, hers, she, he, heaven, heave, eave

PAGE 164

1. b. from the tone of Jeremiah's passionate preaching against the sins of the people.
2. a. from the name of Simon, a convert who asked to buy the gifts of the Spirit (Acts 8:18-19).
3. c. from Judas Iscariot, who betrayed Jesus for thirty pieces of silver (Matthew 27:3).

4. a. from Pilate's action to remove himself from the guilt of condemning Jesus to death (Matthew 27:24).
5. c. from Jesus' teaching that those who follow Him may suffer on account of their beliefs (Luke 14:27).
6. b. from a goat that carried the sins of the people into the wilderness (Leviticus 16:21).
7. a. from Jesus' words referring to faithful witnesses to the Gospel (Matthew 5:13).

PAGE 165

FAITH, BIBLE, LEARN, BREAD, PEACE, POWER
GLORY

The Lord bless thee,
and keep thee.

Numbers 6:24

And let the peace
of God rule in your hearts,
to the which also ye
are called in one body;
and be ye thankful.

Colossians 3:15